# IN THE SUPERMARKET

Dedicated to the memory of
'Corby',
Monsignor Corbishley,
Rector of St Joseph's College,
Mark Cross, 1924–1959,
whose spirituality is reflected here.

TONY CASTLE

# Meeting Christ in the Supermarket

ST PAULS

## ACKNOWLEDGEMENTS

BOOKS:
Bishop Gordon Wheeler, *The Council at a Glance* (Burns and Oates, 1966)
Alfred O'Rahilly, *Merry in God* (Fr William Doyle SJ) (Longmans, Green and Co, London, 1948)
*Autobiography of a Saint, The Story of a Soul* translated by Ronald Knox (Fontana Books, Collins, 1965)
John F.X. Harriott, *The Empire of the Heart* (Templegate-Gracewing, 1990)
Tony Castle, *The Perfection of Love* (Collins, Fount Paperbacks 1986)
John O'Donohue, *Anam Cara* (Bantam Books, London 1997)
Archimandrite Sophrony, *His Life is Mine* (St Vladimir's Seminary Press, New York, 1977)
Eddie Fitzgerald, 'Letting Illness Make the Best of Me' in *Spirituality* (Dominican Publications, Dublin, issue of Nov/Dec 1999)
Eddie Fitzgerald, 'Three Times At Death's Door' *ibid*.
Michel Quoist, *Christ is Alive* (Gill and Macmillan, 1971)

Whilst every effort has been made to contact the copyright holders of extracts used in this book, this has not always been successful. Full acknowledgement will gladly be made in future editions.

ST PAULS Publishing
187 Battersea Bridge Road, London SW11 3AS, UK
www.stpauls.ie

Copyright © ST PAULS 2001

ISBN 085439 601 2

Set by TuKan DTP, Fareham, UK
Printed by Interprint Ltd, Marsa, Malta

ST PAULS is an activity of the priests and brothers of the Society of St Paul who proclaim the Gospel through the media of social communication

## Contents

Introduction 7

Meeting Christ:

| 1. | In the Ordinary | 11 |
| --- | --- | --- |
| 2. | In the Community | 18 |
| 3. | In the Supermarket | 25 |
| 4. | On the Buses | 32 |
| 5. | In the Family | 38 |
| 6. | In the Garden | 44 |
| 7. | Doing the Washing | 52 |
| 8. | At School | 60 |
| 9. | While Decorating | 66 |
| 10. | In the Dole Queue | 72 |
| 11. | In the Park | 78 |
| 12. | In the Surgery | 85 |
| 13. | At Death | 92 |
| 14. | At the War Memorial | 98 |

| 15. | At the Party | 104 |
| 16. | At the Coffee Morning | 109 |
| 17. | On the Internet | 115 |
| 18. | In Children's Books | 122 |
| 19. | At Sunday Football | 129 |
| 20. | Under the Stars | 136 |
| Afterword | | 141 |

# Introduction

It is a very rewarding and refreshing activity to read the first chapter of the Book of Genesis, accompanied by a plain piece of paper and some coloured pencils or crayons (or, if you are a teacher, to use the classroom white board with coloured pens). The story of Creation (chapter 1:1 – chapter 2:3) is very visual and each verse is easy to illustrate. With verse one, the first day of Creation, you start with a light (it has to be modified later) straight line, with dark blue 'water' under the line. Do not attempt any picture of 'the Spirit of God', because, naturally, God is invisible. For verse two, one side of your picture is shaded in, because that is 'night'. You may add the words 'day' and 'night' if you wish.

Verse 6 says 'let there be a vault' (or in the Good News version, 'a dome') separating the waters above the vault, or dome, from those below. So now your picture shows a half circle or dome, above the straight line, with one side of the dome shaded in and the other white and empty; above the dome you colour in the same dark blue 'water'. On the third day, your straight line bulges up, in one or two places (leaving some 'sea'), as you read verse 9, because dry land has appeared! In verse 10 the land 'sprouts' greenery, as you use your artistic skills to draw a few trees, bushes, flowers etc.

Next, on the fourth day, you put a bright yellow sun up in the sky, on the white side; and the moon and stars up on the 'night' side. Day five will test your drawing abilities, because now you need to add birds flying in the sky (sun side) and fish in your sea. This is where my drawing becomes a little 'odd', as I attempt to illustrate a few animals, domestic and wild on the 'land'. And the sixth day is completed by the drawing of man and woman, (in my case, matchstick figures!) among the trees and the animals. And 'God saw all that he had made and it was very good.'

There is a lot to learn from this fun activity. If you were able to draw the picture, what you now have before you is how the people of the Old and New Testaments saw and understood their world: Hebrew cosmology. They were not scientifically educated, as we are, and they only knew what their eyes told them. So the earth is flat and there must be water under the earth, because it bubbles up in springs and streams. There must also be water above the sky, because once or twice a year (not frequently, as we experience in Europe) water pours from the heavens. If people of that time stood in a wide open space – and they had many of those – their eyes told them that the sky touches the land in front of them, behind, and on both sides; so obviously the earth is covered by a great dome. Simple and obvious, if you have only your eye sight to depend upon. So where is God the Creator? That too was obvious to the Hebrew people; he was high above the dome. He looked down on all he had made, and was very pleased with what he saw.

We now know differently, thanks to the work of many astronomers and scientists over the past four hundred years, since the time of Copernicus, Kepler and Galileo. It is interesting, though, that while many modern folk would find Hebrew cosmology quaint and even amusing, they still retain something of it in their religious and spiritual lives. There are still Christians who believe that 'God is up there'; and they direct their prayers up, to an old white bearded figure, beyond 'the dome'!

Modern astronomers tell us that planet earth is one tiny speck in the Milky Way Galaxy, with its billion stars. Out in space there are between one and two hundred billion galaxies and the scientists tell us that the Universe has no end. How can we even begin to imagine that? It is no wonder then that we cannot imagine God, the Creator Spirit, who made all this and holds it in being.

In an earlier book I shared a spiritual experience that had taken me by surprise, when I was a student. I returned, some years ago, to revisit where it had occurred because, simple as it was, it had changed my life. And this book would not exist but for that event.

> There was one place, long and often in my memory, that I particularly wanted to visit. Along the Brickfield Lane I found the place, overgrown, the gate collapsed into the undergrowth, but it was there as I had remembered it, although it was much further from old Rotherfield Station than I had imagined. (It is interesting how our memories often play us tricks about size and distance.) This had been one of our organised class walks, in line, wearing our caps and always in the care of one of the prefects!
>
> In my last year, out with a very small group of seniors, I had stopped at the gate to wait for some slow walkers to catch up. Those I was with wandered ahead a little and I was alone. Then it happened, like a bolt out of the blue. It might be

termed a spiritual experience but for me it was simply that the penny dropped, as we say. I suddenly appreciated something that had escaped me before. It was all at once vividly real and vitally important. 'I live now, not I, but Christ lives in me' (in the Douai version I was accustomed to then) means just what it says. Christ really is within me, now. Christ dwells by faith in my heart. It suddenly became clear, my prayers must not drift up, like incense, into the presence of God, a God away up and out there somewhere. Personal prayer is to the One within.

*Gateway to the Trinity*

The words of St Paul, quoted above, are from his letter to the Galatians, chapter 2, verse 20, and you can find the same teaching in Romans 8:10 and Colossians 2:6. There is a beautiful passage in the first letter of John, chapter 4, especially verses 7-21. John reminds us that 'no one has ever seen God; but if we love one another, God lives in us and his love is made complete in us.'

If my faith tells me that Christ lives within me, then it also tells me that Christ equally lives in others. It is this understanding that alone makes sense of the parable Jesus tells about the Last Judgement; the parable of the Sheep and the Goats (Mt 25:31-46). What we do 'for one of these least brothers' of Christ, we do to or for him. A knowledge of this well-known parable is assumed throughout this book, but is only directly referred to on one or two occasions. (If you, the reader, are not familiar with the parable, please give time to reading and pondering upon its meaning.)

# · 1 ·

# MEETING CHRIST IN THE ORDINARY

I recently came across a slim battered book on the Second Vatican Council, published in 1966. 'The Council at a Glance' pointed out something which has been commonly and widely accepted since, that the most important document to come out of the Council was the Dogmatic Constitution on 'The Church' (This is often known by the title, *Lumen Gentium,* which comes from the two opening words of the document in the original Latin.) The book expressed the opinion that the most important chapter in *Lumen Gentium,* which gave meaning and purpose to the very existence of the Church, was to be found in the centre of that document, chapter five, entitled 'The Universal Call to Holiness'. Many hundreds of thousands of words, over the years, have been written about the contents of the other chapters, but very little about God's call to us all through the words of the Council.

> 'The followers of Christ are called by God, not according to their accomplishments, but according to His own purpose and grace. They are justified in the Lord Jesus, and through baptism sought in faith they truly became children of God and sharers in the divine nature. In this way they are really made holy. Then, too, by God's gifts they must hold on to and complete in their lives this

holiness which they have received... Thus it is evident to everyone that all the faithful of Christ, of whatever rank or status are called to the fullness of the Christian life and to the perfection of love, (para. 40).

After quoting the above, 'The Council at a Glance' continued with these words:

'Therefore it is chapter 5, with its theme of the call to holiness 'through, with and in Christ' which is the axis on which the whole Constitution on the Church revolves'.

Writers and journalists have commented upon the very large number of people, over one thousand, who have been declared to be saints, or beatified, by the Catholic Church in the past twenty years. What is interesting is not so much the number, but who gets included on the list. After an inspection of that list one might be forgiven for coming to the conclusion that to be declared to be of exemplary holiness, a saint, or 'blessed', and worthy of veneration, you must be a bishop, a priest, a monk or a nun; a martyr or the founder of a Religious Order. Lay people, ordinary mums and dads and single people, who make up 90 per cent or more of the Church, do not seem to make it to acknowledged holiness!

Yet our own personal experience tells us differently. Every one of us can think of a member of our family, a friend or an acquaintance who has 'held on to and completed in their lives' the holiness which they received at baptism. For example, the widowed husband or the abandoned wife, who has struggled heroically for years to bring up, single-handed, a family of children; or a parent, or parents, who have sacrificed themselves all day, every day, without respite, to care for a child with very special needs; a wife or husband, who has bravely endured, for many years, a bitterly unhappy marriage in order to provide security for their children. As we journey through life we come upon people whose courage and endurance, in the face of pain and suffering, in so many different guises, have been an incredible and inspiring example of goodness to a wide range of people.

Many years ago, at boarding school, aged sixteen, I read a book that I have never forgotten. *Merry in God* is the life of Fr Willie Doyle, an Irish Jesuit priest who served as a chaplain in the British Army during the First World War. A saintly man, he died heroically (he had several medals for gallantry) trying to minister to a dying soldier in the area known as no-man's land, between the barbed-wire lines of the combatants. His body, mangled by a shell, was never found. I was intrigued not only by the blunt descriptions of the dangerous life of the trenches, but also by Fr Doyle's approach to life and prayer. He records in his diary how he came to see the value and importance of praying, as far as possible, without ceasing. He would repeat, quietly to himself, again and again, throughout the course of the day, hundreds and thousands of short prayers (he calls them 'aspirations'). His method may reflect the devotional age in which he lived, but what interested me at the time was his intention and desire to pray constantly; to be ever in union with Christ.

Our God is a just God. He calls us to holiness, to union with him; but because he is totally fair, loving each one of us with an immeasurable intensity, every human being must have an equal opportunity to answer his call to holiness. God could not make it easy for some, who may have the benefit of a good education, and difficult for others who, for example, have never heard of Christ and Christianity, or simply have absorbing family commitments. (Every human being can choose good, and thereby come close to the fount of all goodness; or follow evil and become separated from God.) Our Father would not call us to something that is not within our reach or capacity to obtain. The Second Vatican Council, writing in this place about Christians, says that holiness is not reserved for any particular group; 'all the faithful of Christ, of whatever rank or status, are called to the fullness of the Christian life.' (Naturally God will provide openings and opportunities appropriate to them, for those outside the Christian family.) If holiness, union with God, is within the reach of everyone, then it does not essentially come from following some religious system or particular spiritual mode of life.

Fr Willie Doyle was undoubtedly very holy and a courageous army chaplain but his way of seeking union with God would not be accessible to most ordinary people.

One young French nun, recently declared a Doctor of the Church, discovered a way that is available to every human being. St Thérèse of Lisieux called it her 'little way'. She desperately wanted to be holy but believed that she was 'too little to do great things'.

> 'I have always found, when comparing myself to the saints, that there is the same difference between them and me as between a mountain with its peak piercing the heavens and the obscure grain of sand trodden underfoot by people in the street.'

She was not put off though; 'instead of getting discouraged, I said to myself, 'God wouldn't inspire me with desires which can't be fulfilled, so in spite of my littleness I shall aspire to holiness.'

Meditating on St Paul's first letter to the Corinthians, chapters 12 and 13, Thérèse found her calling and her 'way'. It was that which is central to all human life; that which is available to every person, of whatever gender, age, nationality, social background or education: the way of love.

> Love, in fact, is the vocation which includes all others; it's a universe of its own, comprising all time and space – it's eternal. Besides myself with joy, I cried out: 'Jesus, my Love! I've found my calling and my calling is love.'

St Thérèse was, of course, reinforcing and developing the teaching of Jesus. According to the teaching of the Jewish religious teachers, with whom Jesus clashed, holiness was reserved to the Jews. They taught that you became holy by keeping exactly the minutiae of the hundreds of rules found in the Torah and in rabbinical interpretations. Jesus told the rabbinical teachers that it was love of God and love of neighbour that brought union with God, for 'all the Law and the Prophets hang on these two commandments' (Mt 22:37-40). It is not easy to love God with 'all your heart and with all your soul and with all your mind' or 'love your neighbour as yourself', but it is accessible to every human being. Every normal human person has the capacity to give and receive love. It is the use and the direction given to that love which decides the acquiring or not of holiness.

At the Last Supper, according to John, chapter 15, Jesus delivered a final farewell homily or discourse to his friends. He speaks, movingly, of the close union in love that he prays will exist between himself and his followers, whom he insists on calling 'friends'.

'As the Father has loved me, so have I loved you.

Now remain in my love' (verse 9). How do we remain in his love? How do we follow 'the little way' of St Thérèse and follow our calling to love? How do we come 'to the fullness of the Christian life and to the perfection of love'?

We use the ordinary. We use what is already there, present in each routine, normal day. Each morning we wake to a new day, and we are already presented with a gift. There are those, people we can all recall, who have run out of days; there are people who finished yesterday, but will not start a new one. No new day should be taken for granted, however routinely boring it might appear. Before us stretches, not just minutes and hours, but countless small actions, heartbeats, breaths, thoughts and so on. Each is a potential gift or act of love. At the start of each day, and as often as we can during that day, we can offer all, and I mean 'all', to the Father, through Christ. 'Father', we can say, 'in union with the wonderful love your Son has for you, I offer you this day. Every thought, every word, every step I take, every touch of my hands, everything is for you; offered in love.' Then, and it takes some effort and practice, we can recall that offering in quiet moments; renew it and be conscious that what I am doing now, whether it is walking down the street, washing up the breakfast things, watching television or sending an e-mail, is done in love.

> 'Whatever you do, whether in word or deed, do it all in the name of the Lord Jesus, giving thanks to God the Father through him' (Col 3:17).

**READING:**

There is no unbridgeable gulf between the Holy One and anyone; in fact, he is closer to us than we are to ourselves. And, as we have already learnt, it was in longing for each of us to be holy that he created each one of us. It follows, as the night the day, that holiness is the normal condition of human kind – in the sense that it is the norm: it is what each of us is meant to be. And since we also know that we are meant to earn our living by the sweat of our brows and by bringing up the next generation of human beings it again follows that our everyday life is the gift by means of which we are meant to draw ever nearer to holiness. Our daily life is the matter, so to speak, which we are meant to transform into holiness.

Donald Nicholl, *Holiness*

**PRAYER:**

> Holy Father, you live in
> unapproachable light and mystery,
> yet you want me to be like you, holy!
> That's a tough one to grapple with.
> 'Holy', is for priests and nuns
> and the pious sort who are always in church.
> I'm not good like them – as you know,
> – thank you for your forgiveness.
> I am grateful for the times
> when I have been aware of your closeness,
> of your loving kindness and care.
> If I've so far failed to be
> the sort of person you want me to be;
> please help me, because without you
> I can do nothing.

## · 2 ·

## Meeting Christ in the Community

The phone rang just after 3.30 in the morning; as I stumbled out of bed and found my way to the kitchen to answer it, I knew who it would be. I wasn't disappointed; it was Rose telling me that Pat, her husband, was having another violent turn. She was terrified of being alone with him. I told her to stay where she was, in her lounge, ignore his calls from the bedroom and I would be round to her in about ten minutes.

This was a call arising from my duties as a Pastoral Lay Assistant in our parish community. There are three PLAs, each with part of the parish as a pastoral area to care for. Our role is to assist the parish priest, who is now the only priest for a large parish, with three distinctly different parts. My area is my own neighbourhood, comprising the large village of Great Wakering. Although the population is almost seven thousand, there are few churchgoers in the village and only about 2 percent are Catholics.

Rose and Pat, both in their early eighties were regular church members, although Pat was bedridden with terminal cancer. Rose tried, as best she could, to care for him in a Council retirement bungalow, which had not been cleaned for a very long time. I had taken Pat Holy Communion myself each Sunday for some time, because I had a good relationship with the couple and felt that I could not ask anyone else to enter their rather unhealthy home. As I would call, from time to time, to take Rose to various church services and events, and pop in to see Pat, I knew all about his occasional, irrational and violent outbursts. (We later learnt, once the Marie Curie nurses took charge, that these were due to a misapplication by Rose, of Pat's medication.)

When I arrived at the bungalow I calmed Rose down first and then went into the bedroom to have a word with Pat. He stopped hammering his walking stick on the bedroom wall when he saw me, but insisted, very loudly, that Rose had been trying to steal his money from under the mattress! He quietened down, but I decided to call out the emergency doctor. The difficulty was in keeping the two apart until the doctor arrived! After the doctor's administrations, including a mild sedative for Rose, who was made comfortable on the settee, I promised to stay until morning. When it was light, at about 7.30 a.m., with calm and pleasant relationships restored, I went home to freshen up to go to work.

With fewer and fewer priests, lay people, like our Pastoral Lay Assistants, are called upon to provide Christian care in the neighbourhood. My colleagues have similar stories to tell, although fortunately they do not occur too often.

There are many different roles played by religious sisters and lay people in our parish, as in most parishes. In addition to the PLAs, there are the three parish sisters who have a roving brief, visiting the sick in the district hospital, preparing children who attend state schools for the sacraments, giving special support to poor families etc. There is the parish Master of Ceremonies (MC) who helps the parish priest in the planning of the liturgy, in which the PLAs and Religious sisters also play a part, along with the choir and the parish musicians. There are the parish catechists who annually prepare the young children for their First Holy Communion, the young people for Confirmation and parents for Baptism. There is the finance committee, the women's group, the Justice and Peace group and so it goes on. No role or group is more important than any other. No group or individual should think of themselves 'more highly than they ought, but rather with sober judgement, in accordance with the measure of faith'; as St Paul reminds us in his letter to the Community at Rome (12:3). He continues:

> 'Just as each of us has one body with many members, and these members do not all have the same function, so in Christ we who are many form one body and each member belongs to all the others. We have different gifts, according to the grace given us.'

St Paul then itemises a list of roles or functions in the community and concludes with these words: 'let him do it cheerfully' (verse 9).

One of the greatest of the Russian Orthodox icon painters was Andrei Rublev. His work dominated the golden age of Russian iconography, in the fourteenth and fifteenth centuries. He is honoured by the Russian Church as St Andrew and was a man of exceptional spiritual vision, with which was combined an outstanding artistic talent. His most famous icon is well known in the West and is often misnamed 'The Old Testament Trinity'; its correct name is 'The Hospitality of Abraham'. This icon, which is familiar to many, shows three angels sitting round a table, on which can be seen a chalice. Icon painters are only allowed, by the strict rules of iconography, to paint historical people or events. This usually means biblical personages, like St John the Baptist, or events, like the Coming of the Holy Spirit on Pentecost Day. In Rublev's famous icon the event painted is that which is found in Genesis chapter 18: the visit to Abraham of three angelic travellers. The text records that this took place 'near the great trees of Mamre', and you can see a great tree in the background of the icon.

Rublev was not the first to paint this biblical scene as an icon, but he developed it in a most skilful and beautiful way to help us to meditate upon the mystery of the Holy Trinity. The 'family' of the three persons round the table, with their loving glances at each other, is set in a perfect circle; representing the circle of love which ideally exists in the human family.

Christianity is a community faith. We are baptised in the name of that Trinity of persons, the Father, the Son and the Holy Spirit; we are caught up into the intimacy of their circle of unending love. To be baptised is to be an adopted child of God and brothers and sisters of one another.

> 'Because you are sons, God sent the Spirit of his Son into our hearts, the Spirit that calls out, *Abba, Father*' (Gal 4:6).
>
> 'How great is the love the Father has lavished on us, that we should be called children of God! And that is what we are!' (1 Jn 3:1).

On Pentecost Day, immediately after the first Christian sermon, delivered by Peter (Acts 2:14-40) many of the crowd respond by accepting baptism. It was the birthday of the Church, for 'about three thousand were added to their number that day.' Their first action was to live in community; 'all the believers were together and had everything in common.' From the first it was understood that to be a Christian meant being a member of a community. It is not long before the community of believers is being identified, by St Paul, as 'the body of Christ'. This is an ever recurring theme throughout his letters:

> 'In Christ we who are many form one body, and each member belongs to all the others' (Rom 12:4).

> 'For we were all baptised by one Spirit into one body – whether Jews or Greeks, slave or free – and we were all given the one Spirit to drink' (l Cor 12:12).

> 'Speaking the truth in love, we will in all things grow up into him who is the Head, that is Christ. From him the whole body, joined and held together by every supporting ligament, grows and builds itself up in love, as each part does its work' (Eph 4:15-16).

Community is the Christian answer to the rampant and damaging individualism of our age. In community Christian demands can be placed upon us that we could otherwise avoid; and hence not grow in love, as we are called to. A priest friend founded and developed in his parish a community-building exercise which involved meetings and, occasionally, a house Mass in neighbours' homes. Two Catholic families lived next door to one another. One went every Sunday to the 9.00 a.m. Mass and the other to the 11.30 a.m. They had not spoken to one another for four years; and refused to speak to one another. The rift, which had not been healed, was over damage to a garden fence!

The parish priest called on the Brownes and asked them to have a House Mass in their home. At first they readily agreed, until the priest asked them to invite all their Catholic neighbours; then they thought of reasons why it would not, after all, be convenient. The priest spoke in general terms about how we are all members of Christ's community and the need we have to accept one another in love. He asked them not make a firm decision now, but to think and pray about it and he would return in a week to see if perhaps it might still be possible. Three days later Mrs Browne called at the priest's house and told the parish priest that she had been round to see her neighbour; they had made up and friendly relations were restored. She would have the House Mass and her neighbour had insisted on helping her to arrange everything.

In community we are faced with challenges like that. In the community we meet Christ for 'God has placed all things under his feet and appointed him to be head over everything for the church, which is his body, the fullness of him who fills everything in every way.' (Eph 1:22).

St Peter, in his first letter, gives good advice to the Christian communities of his day; advice our modern parishes could meditate upon.

> 'Above all, love each other deeply, because love covers over a multitude of sins. Offer hospitality to one another without grumbling. Each one should use whatever gift he has received to serve others, faithfully administering God's grace in its various forms. If anyone speaks, he should do it as one speaking the very words of God. If anyone serves, he should do it with the strength God provides, so that in all things God may be praised through Jesus Christ. To him be the glory and the power for ever and ever. Amen' (4:8-11).

**READING:**

The need for friendship with other persons which most human beings feel is not, in its roots, a sign of weakness but a sign of health. It is not something to be ashamed of but something to delight in, as one delights in the taste of reality. One has to emphasise this truth precisely because certain religious traditions would have us believe that the need for friendship *is* a sign of weakness and that the holier a person becomes the less he needs other persons, until finally he is completely self-sufficient like an Olympian god, needing no other. That such traditions are misguided seems obvious from what we have already said, but it becomes crystal-clear in the light of the Christian doctrine of the Trinity. According to that teaching, ultimate reality is Three-Personed, the perfect union of Father, Son and Holy Spirit. For the human person holiness means sharing ever more fully in that divine friendship.

> Donald Nicholl, *Holiness*

**PRAYER:**

> To belong to a really loving family unit, wonderful!
> And, Father, you've got that, all the time and for ever.
> To exist – is that the right word? – in a never-ending
>     circle of love,
> what an incredible experience!
> Every human being would love to share that.
> Baptism – that was a long time ago –
> gave me a share in your divine life
> and membership of the family of Christ's friends.
> Lord, I've forgotten what dignity
> comes from Baptism.
> Each of us is an adopted child of God;
> we've been drawn into your intimate circle,
> your family of love – what a privilege;
> and we forget it!
> Please shake us all up, Lord;
> bring us to a fresh understanding
> of your community of love,
> of our own community of love
> and the dignity of Baptism.

## · 3 ·

## MEETING CHRIST IN THE SUPERMARKET

One of the wheels on my shopping trolley was wobbly; it was trying to go off in a different direction to the way I was attempting to steer it. It was a battle that I was determined to win and, perhaps as a consequence, has always remained in my memory – my first visit, many years ago, to a supermarket. Nowadays our local supermarket not only has smooth-running vehicles, but a range of alternative models, for mothers with a small baby, or two toddlers and even mini trolleys for young children who demand their own, each equipped with a little flag pole and flag, presumably to assist recovery of a wandering youngster. Most mothers of young children would rather shop alone, but very many have little opportunity for this, so from their earliest years children are initiated into the rites and rituals of the supermarket.

At the time of Jesus, children, especially the girls, would have been initiated into the mysteries of bread-making, weaving, water collecting etc. But even then there would have been the occasional visit to the local market. Nazareth, with a probable population of about two thousand, would have had a market-place where local produce and wares would have been displayed for sale: locally grown olives; grapes, in season; woven baskets and potter's wares. Along with the synagogue, which was probably just off the market area, it was the place where people gathered. Children played there (Lk 7:32) and there too men were hired for a day's labouring(Mt 20:3).

A priest, who has worked in Ghana for many years with street children, came to speak at our school. Fr Patrick asked the class if they liked his brown tweed jacket. He told them that he had bought it second-hand at the 'bend-down boutique'. The children were puzzled, until he explained that in the developing countries of Africa the goods for sale in the market place are laid out to view on the ground; and that is where he saw his jacket. The simple, ancient manner of display still continues in Third World markets. The nearest equivalent in Europe is probably the Boot Fair.

In the Nazareth 'bend-down' market the few locally grown and produced items for sale would seem very dull and impoverished to us. As the village was poor there would be no luxury goods, as people only purchased what they really needed. If goods of any quality were required they would have had to walk the twenty-five miles to Capernaum, where the Great Road brought in traders from the North and the South; but then they would have had to haggle for the goods in Greek.

In the early 1980s, when social and economic conditions were still strictly controlled in Poland and household necessities were in short supply, our family sent parcels of such items to a Polish family of Bielsko-Biala. Barbara, a neighbour of theirs, took it into her head come to England. She turned up at our door, unannounced, and asked if she could stay with us, while she got work and then found herself a flat! She stayed with us for three months, until she returned to Poland with money she had earned from cleaning etc. The day after Barbara arrived we took her with us on our weekly excursion to the local supermarket. As we entered her face was a picture of wonder and astonishment. After ten minutes she turned to me and said, in her broken English, 'It is too much, too much, I have a headache… please take me back.' So I left my duty of pushing the trolley and drove her home. It was such a culture shock for her; she had never seen such variety and such a vast quantity of colourful products before.

It is the staggering variety of goods from all over the world – along with its convenience – that makes the supermarket so appealing. For example, to walk through the fruit and vegetable department, picking up this fruit and that, is a lesson in geography. Avocados from South Africa, melons from Israel, peaches from the USA, bananas from Jamaica, pineapples from Costa Rica, pears from Italy and so it goes on and on.

I have observed the obvious; people do not dress for the supermarket. They pop in, as they are, after taking the children to school; on the way home from work; on the way to the gym; on a Saturday morning in their gardening clothes and so on. Turning into an aisle you may literally bump into a friend, but it is more likely to be a total stranger. In one of the big cities it could be a celebrity, because, as we know from the media, the rich and famous are known to don jeans and dark glasses and pop into their local store. People of all ages, social backgrounds and cultures can be found in the supermarket, its clientele is truly catholic. It reminds me of the Christian Church which is catholic, in other words, universal, open to all and for all, regardless of gender, race, social class or age.

To return to first century Palestine and the marketplace at Nazareth, there would have been no Gentiles in that market-place and gender roles were very clearly defined. The rich, if there had been any living in that area, would have sent their slaves to shop. Yesua Bar Joseph (the real name of Jesus of Nazareth; 'Yesua' is derived from the common name, 'Joshua', and widely used among the Jews of that period) would have known the market-place well, having played there as a child. No one seeing Yesua (or Joshua) in that market-place, as he grew up and matured, would necessarily have noticed anything extraordinary about him. They certainly would not have recognised him as God's anointed, the Messiah (or in Greek, the Christ). He was just another of the village's young men. Only later, after his preaching and miracles, does Simon Peter declare, 'You are the Christ' (Mt 16:16).

Having the allotted task of pushing the trolley, while my wife is engaged in filling it, with just the occasional request for an opinion, I am generally free to observe other shoppers. I see the frail elderly woman, short-sightedly inspecting the half-price special offers; the harassed young mother trying to cope with two irritable young children, while pushing a trolley and selecting from the shelves; the in-love young couple, who are clearly living together and consult one another endlessly about every item, before placing it carefully in their trolley; the experienced middle-aged matron, dutifully followed by her sullen male partner, walking two paces behind. These are my neighbours. These are the people Jesus asks me to love. I observe and have no particular feelings about them; apart from sadness at the sight of the shuffling old lady and amusement at the toddler who, sitting in a trolley, throws items out the moment his mother's back is turned. Surely, if I am to love, I should 'feel' something for them. But no, the love the New Testament writers speak of: the love that Jesus asks for, is *agape*; one of the four Greek words for 'love'. The Greek language is one of the richest of all languages and it has an unrivalled power to express shades of meaning. Just as well, because English is so unrefined, using one word for a whole range of emotions and attitudes. The Gospel writers realised that Jesus, who preached in Aramaic, did not mean *eros,* physical sexual love, nor *storge,* family affection, nor even *philia,* the love found in friendship. Christ constantly asked his followers to 'love your neighbour' (Mt 22:39) and 'love your enemies' (Mt 5:44) and the Greek word the evangelists used was *agape*. A word which is more to do with the mind than the heart; a word which has supremely to do with the will. This 'love' is having a respect for someone, caring about them; we do not have to like someone to accord them respect and be concerned for their welfare. You can 'care' about someone without having any emotions; in fact if we actively dislike someone, Jesus still asks us to love them, in this *agape* sense. We've got it wrong if we think there is a heavenly reward for loving our friends; Jesus clearly says (Lk 6:32) 'if you love those who love you, what credit is that to you?' So we get no reward for following our feelings, only for positively choosing to respect and care for the neighbour who is a stranger or unlovable.

How am I going to love my fellow shoppers? Must I wait until one of them needs a service, then offer a helping hand? For example, an elderly woman tripped over a curb in the supermarket car park recently and broke her hip. Fortunately my wife was alongside her at the time and got her the aid she needed. If I have to wait for something like that to happen, hopefully I would have to wait a very long time. How can my love be real and active *now*?

Each of those I have observed, and all the many

others, have a story, hidden from the human eye. The frail elderly woman, for example, may live alone and be terrified that she is losing her sight; her sons, perhaps, live far away and have not been in touch for a long time. She needs my prayers. The harassed young mother might have been abandoned by her partner and is struggling, on income support, to bring up the children alone; she is constantly so tired-out and desperate that thoughts of ending it all come into her head just too often. She needs my prayers. The domineering middle-aged matron may be putting on a front, she is deeply worried that the lump she has found on her chest is cancerous and she is too frightened to even admit it to herself. She needs my prayers. I can pray too that the young couple's infatuation with one another will grow into a mature love that will last a lifetime.

I do not know of course, each shopper's real physical, moral or spiritual needs, but I do know that they have them and they will benefit from prayer. There is no one who does not need praying for. This is how, secretly, I can love them.

Christ was never recognised in Nazareth's marketplace. When he visited its synagogue, at the start of his preaching ministry, he read a prophecy about the Messiah, from Isaiah (Lk 4:18) and then commented, 'today this Scripture is fulfilled in your hearing.' The devout Jews of Nazareth recognised him as a local lad and knew well enough what he was claiming. And they threw him out! They were so outraged that they even tried to kill him.

With the eyes of faith we can, today, do better; we can recognise Christ in our local supermarket. Did he not say, 'what you do for the least of my brothers and sisters, you do for me' (Mt 25:40)?

**READING:**

O Christ, in this man's life
This stranger who is Thine – in all his strife,
All his felicity, his good and ill
In the assaulted stronghold of his will;

I do confess Thee here,
Alive within this life; I know Thee near
Within this lonely conscience, closed away
Within this brother's solitary day.

Christ in his unknown heart,
His intellect unknown, this love, this art,
This battle and this peace, this destiny
That I shall never know, look upon me.

Christ in his numbered breath,
Christ in his beating heart and in his death,
Christ in his mystery! From that secret place,
And from that separate dwelling, give me grace!

Alice Meynell, *The Unknown Christ*

**PRAYER:**

Father, the people you have created
are so interesting.
In the supermarket you can see
so many interesting replicas of You.
You have made us in your image –
and it is such a rich assortment!
Does it really matter what we look like?
Isn't it the heart that counts?
And what state are these,
my neighbours' hearts in?
Lord, I know that I need prayer;
so I must assume that each of my neighbours
needs prayer too.
Father, may I recognise your Son
in each and every one.
As your Son is close to your heart,
please keep these my neighbours,
and their every need,
close to your loving heart.

## · 4 ·

## Meeting Christ on the Buses

Every working day I catch the 7.32 a.m. bus from opposite the old Norman village church. Frequently I have to run down our road to the corner and, once in a while, I miss it. Whatever the weather the fifteen-minute wait for the next one seems long and a waste of time, but then with a hiss of brakes the number 5 comes around the corner and pulls up; the wait is forgotten. I settle down to read and twenty minutes later I'm in town and waiting at the next stop for the shorter final leg of the journey. It is relatively smooth and untroubled; the return journey in the afternoon is a different story! The buses are rarely on time and, when you are tired after a hectic day, the waiting, sometimes in the wet and cold, is very trying.

One winter's afternoon I was standing patiently in the bus queue when three teenage girls came along, saw me and stopped to talk. They were pupils from the High School where I teach. They opened the conversation with a surprised, 'Sir, is it you?' I confirmed that it was. 'What are you doing here?' I answered that, surprisingly, I was waiting for a bus. It was they who were clearly surprised. 'Haven't you got a car?' one asked; another added, 'the other teachers have cars.' I explained that as a family we possessed a car but my wife had the use of it during the day. The girls' expressions showed how sorry they felt for me and, after a few more pleasantries, they wandered off. Most of our pupils come from comfortable backgrounds and are accustomed to being ferried everywhere by car; public transport is for the poor. That exchange made me wonder, not for the first time, whether I should get a Mini Metro or some other small car, just to travel to and from school in comfort. But once again I rejected the notion, because there are already too many cars on the road and if, in some very small way, I could have a sense of solidarity with the struggling poor of the developing nations, who are forced to wait for many hours, for uncomfortable rides in clapped-out transport, that would be no bad thing.

Gazing out the window, as the bus sped up Southchurch Boulevard I recalled how, two years ago, I would briskly walk the six miles home from school, as a training exercise. It would take approximately ninety minutes and it was part of my preparation for the Coast to Coast Walk that I was planning to undertake. The whole Walk from St Bees Head, near Whitehaven, on the Cumbrian coast, across the Cumbrian mountains and the Pennines, to Robin Hood's Bay, near Whitby, on the east coast is a journey of 190 miles. That experience taught me many lessons. One was the hardiness of Jesus and his friends, who walked similar long distances, for example, to and from Jerusalem from the northern province of Galilee.

Long journeys, all of them 'walks', are an important and familiar part of the Old and New Testaments. There is the very long walk of Abraham, and his flocks, from Ur, in modern Iraq, up the valley of the Euphrates to Haran, then west and eventually south to Canaan, modern Israel. The Book of Genesis, 12:5, says simply, 'they set off for Canaan, and arrived there.' A meandering walk, with flocks of camels, sheep and goats, of at least five hundred miles!

Life is a journey. Many writers, poets and hymn writers have compared life, from cradle to grave, to a journey. For Christians, who have faith in a life with God after death, there is a clear, if uncertain, goal to journey towards. The eighteenth-century hymn writer, Anne Steel, wrote:

> Let the sweet hope that thou art mine
> my path of life attend;
> Thy presence thro' my journey shine,
> and crown my journey's end.

and from the pen of a more recent hymn writer, Estelle White:

> Walk with me, oh my Lord,
> through the darkest night
> and brightest day.
> Be at my side, oh Lord,
> hold my hand
> and guide me on my way.

This understanding of life is based upon the teaching of Jesus himself who declared 'I am the Way' (Jn 14:6); 'that you must travel' is understood. From Pentecost Day, the first followers of Jesus were called, not 'Christians', but the 'People of the Way' (Acts 9:2, 19:9). This name for Christ's followers continued until, years later, at Antioch (Acts 11:26), they received the nickname 'Christians'. So my life, as a member of 'the People of the Way', or as a Christian, is a journey made in faith; with the Scriptures as my map and compass; and Christ as my travelling companion. However alluring other paths may be we must always refer to and trust in Christ, who walks with us.

In the New Testament many journeys are recorded; pre-eminently those of the Apostle Paul, who walked hundreds of miles to spread the Good News of Christ. The evangelist Luke ends his Gospel with an important journey; the story of the two disciples walking to Emmaus, on the afternoon of Easter Day (Lk 24:13-35). As the two disciples talk, immersed in current affairs, a stranger joins them, listens to their story and, sensing their lost and confused state, refers them to the Scriptures. Christ walks alongside, shares their troubles; he is very real to them, but they do not recognise him. Then, when they stop and have supper, 'he took bread, gave thanks, broke it and began to give it to them. Then their eyes were opened.' They recognised him in the breaking of bread, but he had been there, with them, all the time!

The Eucharist is much more than a service that we go to at the weekend. Many people have a hard and difficult journey through life. We all have times when the going gets tough; sometimes we stumble and fall; other times we wander off the track and get lost. There are times when we want to give up and feel that we just can't make the effort any more. But whatever happens and however we feel, we have our compass and our map and we have Christ, our travelling companion, ever with us. If we fail to recognise Christ in those we meet each and every day of our earthly journey, will our eyes be opened when we gather with our community for the Eucharist; when our travelling companion becomes our food for the journey; not just alongside us, but within us?

There is an illuminating little story about a walk in the First Book of Kings. The prophet Elijah was in trouble. He had upset Queen Jezebel and had to flee for his life. One day's journey into the desert he felt so miserable that he prayed that he might die.

(1 Kings 19:3-9). He fell asleep, but an angel woke him and insisted that he eat. After a second sleep he was again awakened, the angel saying 'get up and eat, for the journey will be too much for you.' Strengthened by that food he travelled for forty days and forty nights.' Fortified with the regular reception of the Eucharist we too can travel safely and with renewed confidence.

The bus drivers on my number 5 route vary from day to day. However, one of them, Ian, a big bluff middle-aged man, always smart in his uniform, seems to be on duty about every ten days. He is always in good humour and very popular with the regulars on his route. The moment the doors open, he calls out a greeting and passes some jocular remark. 'Good morning, *Sir*, he says to me, emphasising the 'sir' because he knows I am a teacher. Recently on a very beautiful sunny morning he called out to those of us sitting towards the front of the bus, 'Too nice for work today. Who fancies a trip to Brighton?' Much laughter and then people start talking to one another. I heard him reply, when a passenger standing near him commented on his good humour: 'I like turning things around. People get on with long faces, I like them to get off with a smile.' And they do.
    I suspect that Ian has no specific religious affiliation, and he's totally unaware of it but he is Christlike in the thoughtful uplift he gives to people on their journey – not just on that bus ride but their life journey that day. Did not Christ come to 'turn things around'?

**QUOTES TO PONDER:**

Lord Jesus, the way by which we travel: show me yourself, the Truth that we must walk in; and be in me the Life that lifts us up to God, our journey's ending. *Frederick McNutt*

The Godward journey is a journey on which every individual is launched, all unknowingly, at birth. *Christopher Bryant*

May he give us all the courage that we need to go the way he shepherds us, that when he calls we may go unfrightened. If he bids us to come to him across the waters, that unfrightened we may go. And if he bids us climb the hill, may we not notice that it is a hill, mindful only of the happiness of his company. He made us for himself, that we should travel with him and see him at last in his unveiled beauty in the abiding city, where he is light and happiness and endless home. *Bede Jarrett*

**PRAYER:**

> We are always making journeys, Lord,
> so it is easy to understand how,
> in a certain sense, life is a journey.
> It was never your intention that we
> should travel it alone.
> Just as you joined the two disciples,
> on the road to Emmaus, walk with me.
> Just as you opened their eyes to the
> words of the Scriptures, open my eyes too.
> Just as they recognised you
> in the Breaking of Bread, may I regularly
> recognise you in the sacrament of the Eucharist,
> and draw from it my strength for the journey.

## · 5 ·

## MEETING CHRIST IN THE FAMILY

Nowadays we appear to be spared the dreadful mother-in-law jokes that were the stock in trade of the stand-up comedians of yesteryear. My mother-in-law, who is not a churchgoing person, has been, and is, one of the most generous persons you are ever likely to meet. She had only known me a few months when her daughter took me to their home at Christmas-time. Like my own, Liz's people are a down-to-earth working-class family. When the Christmas presents were given out, from under the tree, I was thrilled to receive a brightly-wrapped gift. It was a pair of trousers. A little later, to my surprise, I was handed another gift; it was a shirt and tie to go with the trousers. Then another present, a very fashionable pullover! In all I received five well-chosen parcels from under the tree: And it has always been like that. It should be noted, in passing, that Dilys, my mother-in-law, would work overtime during the year, at her cleaning job, in order to have the money to spend on her family and friends at Christmas. It was rarely spent on herself. Her daughter exhibits the same cheerful generosity.

Some months ago, at 9 p.m. on a Monday evening, our parish priest rang and spoke to my wife. She came into the lounge and, in her brisk manner, said, 'we're having Philip for the night. He might be here for a few days.' Without a moment's hesitation she had agreed to the priest's request that we take the boy in. The parish priest had asked her because he knew that she had generously done this sort of thing more than once before. It transpired that the eight-year-old boy stayed with us for a total of nine weeks. Philip's parents were divorced and he lived with his mother; she had had a serious breakdown and was admitted to the psychiatric wing of the local hospital. The boy had only rarely spent time with his father, who was often out of the country.

A few days after Philip's arrival I made a discovery that I was not expecting. Philip's father, who we had only seen once or twice before, telephoned to ask if he could call at our home and discuss with us when he could see his son. A visiting time was agreed for the following afternoon. Philip was visiting his friend's house at that precise time and was not immediately due back. Mr Kelly arrived and his manner was rather stiff and formal. He asked to speak to me privately in the kitchen. We had hardly begun the conversation when Philip arrived back from his friend's and came in through the kitchen door. The moment he caught sight of his father he looked frightened; his head dropped and he tried to slide along the walls in the direction of the lounge, without looking up. I called Philip over to say 'hello' to his father. He did not want to come near. Mr Kelly looked at him, said 'hello' and turned back to speak to me. Philip, highly relieved, darted off to the lounge.

In the following weeks it was sadly very clear that the father did not know how to relate to his son. The body language was wrong, the father's speech was wrong; he possessed no parenting skills. I am sure that social workers see it all the time, but for me this was a new experience; I had never before witnessed a parent who did not have any idea how to relate to his child.

My new experience brought me a fresh realisation and a greater appreciation of what my parents had done for me. We learn by imitation. The parenting skills that I have, no one formally taught me; I now realise that I picked them up, as I picked up my values and my Christian faith, from my loving parents. How important parents are!

One of the most important qualities that I recognised, almost from the beginning, in the woman, who became my wife, was her spontaneous generosity; caught from her mother and developed by herself. That is an important point, for if we were only mirror images of our parents, we would never act freely. Young people can, and do, reject their parents' values. People, who have a poor start in life, can be heavily influenced by their peers and embrace other values. Frequently, too, young people reject their family's standards, but return to them in later life (as we can see in the lives of some of the great saints, like St Augustine of Hippo). However – if we have been blessed with one – the most powerful influence in all our lives is the family that we are born into and brought up in.

Most Christians first meet Christ in the family, not at church or at school. Usually the latter can only hope to develop and reinforce what already exists; although once in a while young people, not brought up in a Christian home, can come to know Christ through their attendance of a Christian school. Everyone has heard it said that faith is not taught, it's caught. It is the practised faith of parents, parent, or guardian that conveys, without words, a love of Christ.

The family in which Jesus was brought up was no less important for him. There he learnt his Judaism and, humanly, his great love of God. He was totally and completely human and therefore as influenced by his mother and step-father as any one of us. His divinity did not impair or further his human development. He still had to be taught to say his prayers and politely to say 'please' and 'thank you'. He still had to do his Hebrew homework, brought home from his lessons at the local synagogue. We cannot identify what Jesus received from each of those who brought him up, but we might boldly suggest that his manliness, his respect for women and the poor, along with his trade, he learnt from Joseph. His compassion and gentle caring for the sick, his patience with his disciples and his perseverance, he 'caught' from Mary. What he received from either, and both together, we can, at this distance in time, and with what little evidence we have, only guess at. What is certain is that the qualities and values that Jesus imbibed in his home at Nazareth are the very same values and standards that we need to exhibit in our homes.

In the course of human history family life, at this time, has probably never been more difficult, with attacks upon it from all sides. We need to find, and keep, Christ in our homes. Many years ago, an American priest toured Great Britain holding rallies in all the major cities. In London he spoke at a vast Catholic Rally at Wembley stadium. His constant theme, blazoned out on a great banner at Wembley, became a Christian watchword; 'the family that prays together stays together'. While, sociologically, it would be difficult to prove or disprove that assertion, it does have a ring of truth about it. It is certain that families that do pray together find that it gives the family unit a great sense of unity and strength. A famous

New York psychiatrist is reported to have said, 'in forty years of practice, I have never treated anyone who really prayed'. The simplest form of family prayer is grace before meals; not the rattled-off formula which passes for prayer, but a genuine expression of gratitude for the food, for the health and happiness of the family. Such a simple opportunity also provides an opening for a short prayer for any pressing needs.

**READING:**

Love which can exist only in a secret garden soon finds the world knocking down the walls and breaking in. Only a love which is free, frank, proudly acknowledged, can walk through the wilderness of the world unscathed and bring the wild beasts to heel. I think it was Antoine de Saint Exupery who said that love was not looking into each other's eyes, but looking together in the same direction. A Christian couple must look outside themselves, be concerned with, and at the service of others, and in so doing they mysteriously grow together, just as the individual becomes his true self by giving himself away.

John F.X. Harriott, *The Empire of the Heart*

**PRAYER:**

    Couples and families are breaking up,
        all around us, Lord.
    It is frightening, sad and threatening
        Children at school talk easily about
        their dad's girlfriend having a baby!
        Stepmothers and fathers are becoming
        the expected norm.
    Some children have never known a father.
        In this turmoil, is our family life secure, Lord?
        Everyone does it, we are told!

Is it worth keeping up the effort
> to keep temptations at bay?
> Yes, I am sure that's your answer, Lord.
Yes, look not at the mess some people
> have got themselves into, but
> at the faithful happy couples with their families.
See the secure love their children enjoy.
See their children's mature confidence.
Lord, come and be a member of our family,
> that we may know you are there to give us strength
> when the going gets tough.
Give us a share, please, of your strong unselfish love
> that we may put each other before self.
And there when we are proud of our children,
> their achievements and our united family love.

## · 6 ·

## MEETING CHRIST IN THE GARDEN

You can make some strange and important discoveries in gardens. Not long after we had moved into our present semi-detached house, which is 120 years old, I made an unusual discovery in our garden. More accurately what I found was on the edge of a concrete apron, rather like a patio, outside our back door. I took no notice of the rusting rectangular iron manhole cover for some weeks, but then one day curiosity drove me to lift it. I was expecting to see the usual open conjunction of waste pipes, but what met my gaze was a hole full of water. I found a long bamboo runner bean cane and lowered it into the water. It was two metres long and did not touch the bottom. I looked for a longer cane and tried again; this just touched the bottom. My first thought was that I had discovered a well.

My wife, who is a childminder, was very insistent that it had to go! It was far too dangerous to be there, where children constantly played. Whatever its origin and purpose, the questions that interested me, my wife demanded that it be emptied and filled in with rubble. A retired local builder, who had lived all his life in the neighbourhood, told me that it was not a well or a cesspit, but a water cistern. When our house had been built, in the nineteenth century, there was no supply of water from the mains; the cistern was built to store the rain water that came off the roof. Alongside the underground cistern would have been the washhouse and the water was mainly used to wash the family's clothes.

Bucket by slow bucket, the cistern took a long time to empty. When the bucket on my rope was leaning over and dragging on the bottom, I lowered a ladder and went down into the hole with a torch. I was surprised by the quality of the workmanship of the cistern's construction. I found myself standing in a circular underground chamber, as wide as it was deep, with smooth concrete walls and floor. It seemed such a shame to destroy it; I momentarily wondered if it could be converted into a nuclear fallout bunker or a wine cellar! I knew that neither idea would appeal to my practical wife, who only wanted to see it filled in.

I hammered three holes into the floor of the cistern, so that any rain-water gathering there would drain away and then filled it in with a huge mound of hardcore and rubble that I had collected for the purpose. Before starting I left a time capsule on the floor of the cistern; a biscuit tin containing a national newspaper, a local one, coins and stamps of that year and a note accompanying photos of the family. I thought that it might make an interesting discovery for some future explorer of the cistern. The final touch was to build a raised brick flower bed over the old manhole cover.

In a garden, because most of us no longer live in the countryside, you can experience the rhythm of nature's seasons. The start of the gardening year in the spring, with its fresh new life and hope after the barren dead winter months leads to the bright flowers and long evenings of the summer and the mature colours of the autumn. Martin Luther reminds us of the power of nature to draw our minds to things of the Spirit when he writes 'Our Lord has written the promise of the Resurrection, not in books alone, but in every leaf in springtime.'

Events in three gardens are central to the biblical story of our salvation. There is the Garden of Eden, with the event that we call 'The Fall'; there is the Garden of Gethsemane with Christ's agony and prayer; and there is the Garden of the Resurrection and the meeting of the Risen Christ with Mary Magdalene.

The two stories of Creation, found in the first and second chapters of Genesis, contradict one another, but transmit wonderful spiritual and theological messages to us. The oldest of the stories, by about five hundred years, is the second one, which includes the story of the creation of woman from the rib of the man and the temptation of them both in the Garden of Eden. 'Now the Lord God had planted a garden in the east, in Eden; and there he put the man he had formed' (verse 8). So man is placed in the garden 'to work it and take care of it'. Before God provides a helper and companion for the man he gives him a command, 'you must not eat of the tree of the knowledge of good and evil'. The penalty will be death.

Chapter three opens with the talking serpent, identified by Judaism and Christianity as the traditional enemy of mankind, Satan or the Devil, as the great deceiver. Notice that deception precedes temptation. In my own experience this is generally what happens. We convincingly deceive ourselves into believing that this action is all right for me, because… and we have wonderful reasons to justify our action.

The woman 'saw that the fruit of the tree was

good... pleasing... and desirable'. That is the trouble with evil: it does not look bad to the eye of the beholder. Our self-deception makes it look good and desirable. The woman took the fruit and 'gave some to her husband, who was with her, and he ate it'. They were totally disobedient. The simple request and command of God was ignored. Conscience springs into action and hearing God walking in the garden, 'they hid'. They feel exposed to the gaze of God; 'I was afraid' the man says, 'because I was naked; so I hid.' They start blaming one another, just as we often do today; Adam blames Eve and she blames the serpent; but they are all guilty and all must be punished. Pain and death enter and destroy the beautiful work of God's creation. There is a rift between mankind and the Creator. The ingratitude of the creatures, the monstrous pride of the beings made from the dust of the earth has issued in the first, or original, sin of mankind, the sin of disobedience. Only an act of perfect obedience, by someone who can bridge the gulf between creature and Creator, will rectify the relationship.

If you have the opportunity to go to the Holy Land, you will, almost certainly, visit the mount of Olives, a hill, on the eastern side of Jerusalem, opposite the Temple mount. There you will find the Church of All Nations and the traditional site of the prayer and agony of Jesus. Just outside the church you will visit a garden laid out under the ancient twisted olive trees. The Gospels speak of an olive grove and name it 'Gethsemane' (which means 'olive press'). Christian tradition has always honoured this area as 'the Garden of Gethsemane'. Here Jesus came to pray after his last Passover meal with his friends.

In this period of prayer the human nature of Jesus

is very apparent. He tells his disciples that his soul 'is overwhelmed with sorrow to the point of death'. He asks them to keep watch with him. Taking Peter, James and John apart from the others, Jesus then leaves the three to be on his own. 'He fell with his face to the ground and prayed' (Mt 26:39). It is the content of this prayer which is so important for the future of humanity. If Jesus had prayed, 'please help me to cope with the pain that lies ahead of me' that would have shown his dependence upon divine help, but as a good and strong man suffering for his beliefs, and no more. Jesus, however, was much more human and much closer to us in our own experiences. He cried out, pleading with God not to let him suffer. 'You can do anything', he cries in the agony of the moment, 'you can take this suffering away from me. Please take it away; please do not ask this of me' (cf. Mk 14:36).

We do not know how long Jesus struggled, in the darkness of the garden, with this prayer, until he reached the point when he adds the words, 'yet not what I will, but what you will be done.' Like every one of us, who do all we can to avoid pain, Jesus pleaded to be spared; but he came to accept that it was the express will of God. In complete obedience he accepts his Father's will, and all that that will entail. In the words of St Paul 'he humbled himself and became obedient to death – even death on a cross' (Phil 2:8).

Jesus, who was both human and divine, gave to God the complete obedience that Adam and Eve failed to give. Paul, the great thinker and theologian of the first century of Christianity, spells out clearly the implications of Christ's obedience and sacrifice of his own self-will. His teaching can be found in two of his letters; that to the Christians of Rome and his first letter to the Christian community at Corinth.

> 'If, by the trespass of the one man' (Paul has already spoken of Adam), 'death reigned through that one man, how much more will those who receive God's abundant provision of grace and of the gift of righteousness reign in life through the one man, Jesus Christ' (Rom 5:17).

> 'Just as through the disobedience of the one man the many were made sinners, so also through the obedience of the one man the many will be made righteous' (verse 19).

At Easter time many local parish churches construct an Easter garden in the church, as part of the seasonal decorations. Some go to great lengths to use these as teaching aids.

One Easter, in our village Methodist church, a garden was laid out towards the front of the church and the youth group presented a living tableau. It worked well and was a very memorable effort. The information that the tomb of Jesus, a burial chamber built for the rich Joseph of Arimathea, was in a garden, comes from John's Gospel.

> 'At the place where Jesus was crucified, there was a garden, and in the garden a new tomb, in which no-one had ever been laid' (Jn 19:41).

Two events occurred in that garden: the burial chamber was found to be empty and Jesus was seen by Mary Magdalene, who at first mistook him for the gardener. The first is fact, acknowledged by both the friends and enemies of Christ. The second is faith. On the third day, after the gift of Christ's complete obedience, God the Father rewarded that obedience by raising him. As Simon Peter proclaimed in the first ever Christian sermon (Acts 2:32), 'God has raised this Jesus to life, and we are all witnesses of the fact…

let all Israel be assured of this; God has made this Jesus, whom you crucified, both Lord and Christ' (verse 36). The total obedience of Jesus, prompted by his limitless love, is rewarded by his Father.

St Paul sums it up very neatly, and applies it to our own futures:

> 'Christ has indeed been raised from the dead, the first fruits of those who have fallen asleep. For since death came through a man, the resurrection of the dead comes also through a man. For as in Adam all die, so in Christ all will be made alive' (1 Cor 15:20-22).

In our family garden the underground chamber could not be left empty, it had to be filled in. In the Easter garden Christ's empty tomb is worthless to us unless we 'fill in' what is necessary; our faith and total acceptance of Christ's living presence with us. His love and obedience more than inspire us, they provide us with the model that the Father wishes us to imitate.

**READING:**

If we are willing, every moment of our lives can resound with the joy of Easter. And the true Christian cannot live without joy. Through Christ, he encounters joy and lives in joy. He is given over to joy. In his life there can be no enduring failure – neither suffering nor death are insurmountable obstacles for him. Everything is the raw material of redemption, of resurrection, for, in the middle of his sufferings and his deaths, Christ the Conqueror waits.

By 'joy' we do not mean the transient pleasure... but rather the calm, the interior serenity, and the profound peace which permeate and emanate from a person who, notwithstanding a torn heart and body, and despite the suffering of mankind and the world, believes with all his strength in the victory of the Saviour.

The person who has entered into this joy and remains in it becomes, in Christ, what the Father wants him to be. He has reached his true level, as a person who is totally developed; for he has reached the ultimate stage in his communion with the Mystery of Jesus - not only the mystery of Creation; not only the mystery of the Incarnation; not only the mystery of the Redemption. But also the mystery of Resurrection.

Michel Quoist, *Christ is Alive*

**PRAYER:**

I love gardens, Lord.
Who was it that said:
'one is nearer God's heart in a garden
than anywhere else on earth'?*
Well, it is true that all the great
spiritual events happened in gardens.
Mankind's fall, Christ's acceptance
of his Father's will
and the Resurrection; all in gardens.
Winter and Spring,
Night and Dawn.
Falling and getting up again,
Dying and rising.
The Easter rhythm to life.
Help me, Lord, to seek
and find your will for me.
Help me, Lord, please,
to get up every time that I fall;
and the strength to try again.
Grant that, eventually, when I die,
I may rise again, with Christ. Amen

---

* Dorothy Gurney, *The Lord God Planted a Garden*.

· 7 ·

# Meeting Christ Doing the Washing

Modern technology has probably done more for the weekly clothes wash in the home than for any other family chore. For one thing it is no longer a weekly event, occupying many hours of hard labour, but, in a busy home, a daily occurrence. Washing clothes, as the need arises, at the touch of a button, is a simple and speedy operation. This change has altered how everyone thinks about clothes and fashion.

In the late 1940s when, as a child, I lived for a while with my grandparents, I witnessed the old process of the weekly wash, the pattern of which, I suspect, had not changed for centuries. In the corner of my Grandma's stone-flagged kitchen was a brick-built copper. There was an aperture on the floor level for a fire to be laid and a wooden lid on the top, which covered the water as it boiled. Nearby stood the large iron-framed mangle, with solid wooden rollers. This, of course, was used to squeeze the water out of the clothes once they had been boiled, scrubbed on the washboard and boiled again. Modern fabrics would not survive such a mangling! I shall never forget my Gran's joy when my parents treated her, for her birthday one year, to a neater, smoother modern mangle that had rubber rollers! In those days the family wash took three days of hard work. My Grandmother would get up early on a Monday morning to lay and light the fire under the copper. Then she would fill the copper, bucket by bucket, with cold water (there was no other kind). Later she would add the soda crystals as the water began to boil and sort the 'whites' from the 'coloureds' – each to be washed separately. When the time was right, items of the wash were extracted steaming from the copper to receive a scrubbing on the washboard. And so the lengthy process continued until it was time to hang them outside to dry. The next day the ironing would start, using a pair of irons heated on the kitchen range. It was three days of hard work; all to be repeated again four days later.

Mary of Nazareth must have faced a similar weekly chore, although, of course, the clothes would not have been ironed. Once Jesus left home and travelled around the countryside preaching and healing, you wonder how he and his companions got their clothes washed! A down-to-earth thought, but to understand the work and role of Jesus it is necessary to keep him rooted in the real world. There are so many misconceptions about. In a recent classroom play a student, taking the part of Jesus, walked around the whole time with her arms out from her sides with her palms facing upwards. When I asked why she was doing this, Natalie explained that she thought that was what Jesus did. It must be right, she explained indignantly, because she had seen a statue in her church showing him like that. One wonders how many other people have similar misguided ideas about Jesus.

Modern Israel is not a country just inhabited by the Jews. It is a multi-cultured, multi-faith land. Not only are there several different ways of living the Jewish Faith, there are different divisions of Christianity and at least two ways of practising the

Islamic Faith. At the time of Jesus it was not very different. There were several different Jewish parties or groups; for example, the Pharisees, the Sadducees and, out in the wilderness, the Essenes.

There were people of Greek extraction and retired Roman soldiers, who had married local girls, living in towns built, like Scythopolis (Bet Shean), on the Greek model. This city, at the time of the Roman occupation, had a bigger population than Jerusalem and was only twenty-five miles from Nazareth; yet it is never mentioned in the Gospels.

Scholars, in recent years, as a result of the discovery of the Dead Sea Scrolls, near the north-west shore of the Dead Sea in the late 1940s, have learnt much more about the Jewish sect known as the Essenes. Apart from references to them in the writings of Pliny, Josephus and Philo, little was known until their writings and the remains of their community settlement at Wadi Qumran, a type of monastery, were discovered. What was particularly fascinating about the community quarters was the network, within one building, of waterways linking seven large cisterns, where water was stored. These were for their regular ritual washings or baptisms. The members of the community were celibates, keeping themselves pure as they awaited not one, but two Messiahs; a kingly one and a priestly one.

It is not unlikely that the place on the banks of the Jordan, where John the Baptist, started preaching and then baptising people, was the very spot where the local women came to do their weekly wash. John would have needed a first audience, to get started. The women would then have returned to their neighbouring settlements with the message that a new prophet had appeared on the banks of the Jordan, looking rather like Elijah (compare 2 Kings 1:8 with Mark 1:6). That news would have brought out the crowds.

When asked if he were the Christ, John declared that the Messiah would soon be among them. In preparation for his appearing, 'Repent' he said and show you are truly sorry by accepting baptism in the waters of the Jordan. Interestingly, John was baptising some fifteen miles from the site of the desert community at the Wadi Qumran.

Luke says that 'the word of God came to John, son of Zechariah in the desert' (3:2). Where in the desert? At Qumran? Had John been a member of that baptising community? That question is of considerable interest but unanswerable.

John told the crowds that the best preparation that they could make, for the arrival of the Christ, the anointed of God, was to reject sin and assume responsibility for their past bad actions. 'What should we do?' the crowd asks; then the tax collectors ask 'what should we do?'; even the soldiers in the crowd ask, 'what should we do?' John does not want his listeners to just regret and be sorry for past sins, important as this is, but to assume responsibility for what they have done and, in the future, act differently. John is announcing that the final age has come, when we must maturely accept responsibility for our own sins and not lay them on scapegoats.

Several years ago, when I had the opportunity of spending a week in Cracow, Poland, I was taken by a Polish priest to visit the birth place of Pope John Paul II. The country bus dropped us off in the market place of the sleepy little town of Wadowice. Within a few minutes we were standing in the church of Our Lady, admiring the font in which Karol Wojtyla was baptised. The stout Polish parish priest appeared and invited us into his presbytery; with great pride he opened a safe and took out a baptismal register, covering the years, 1917-1927. At the foot of page 549 there was the entry. On 18 May 1920, Karol Jozef Wojtyla, son of Karol and Emilia, received the sacrament of Baptism. In another space, alongside, his ordination to the priesthood on 1 November 1946, is recorded. This entry confidently occupies most of the space; squeezed in underneath is the date of his consecration as bishop. Along the bottom margin is recorded when he was elevated to Cardinal and finally, in the last remaining part of the margin, it says, 'On 16 October 1978, he was elected Pope, assuming the name John Paul II.' The point is inadvertently, but clearly made; the most important event in the life of Karol Wojtyla was his baptism. The waters of the font, the sign of the gift of new life, the receipt of adoptive sonship, bestowed something greater than the ordination, consecration and election that followed in later life.

My grandmother had to repeat the heavy work of the weekly wash, taking from Monday to Wednesday, week after week. Of course, even with the luxury of the modern machine it remains a continual boring chore. The Essenes at the time of Jesus ritually washed themselves again and again in their baptismal cisterns. There is nothing to suggest that, in imitation of this, those whom John baptised did not return again and again. In stark contrast, Christian baptism is once and for all; unrepeatable. St Paul points out in his letters that it is faith in Christ and baptism into his death and resurrection that unites us with Christ and one another.

> 'Don't you know that all of us who were baptised into Christ Jesus were baptised into his death? We were therefore buried with him through baptism into death in order that, just as Christ was raised from the dead through the glory of the Father, we too may live a new life' (Rom 6:3).

Baptism destroys all that divides; it unites us all into one body,

> 'All of you who were baptised into Christ have clothed yourselves with Christ. There is neither Jew nor Greek, slave nor free, male nor female, for you are all one in Christ Jesus' (Gal 3:28).

so that we should all,

> 'Make every effort to keep the unity of the Spirit through the bond of peace. There is one body and one Spirit - just as you were called to one hope when you were called – one Lord, one faith, one baptism' (Eph 4:3).

Just as washing ourselves and our clothes is a continual and regular event, so is dying and rising again. We are baptised, just once, into the death and resurrection of Christ. It does not need repeating, but our baptism calls us to, and places upon us, the duty to make the constant effort to 'die' to our selfishness and sin and 'rise' to a new life. Daily we sin, (let's call it what it is!), often in such small ways; but Christ calls us to holiness and closer and more personal union with him. Daily we need to acknowledge our failings, ask for forgiveness and start again. The joy of it is, that no matter at what stage of the process we are at – dying or rising – Christ is continually with us, as our brother, through baptism.

**READING:**

All the sacraments are an answer to the plea of God's children: Let me hold it, let me touch. They continue the process of making his power and presence visible, which began when he came among us as a visible man. There is nothing superstitious in the Church's understanding of these signs. They do not deny the possibility that God can and may act upon us directly in ways not visible to the senses and without working through human instruments. But for human beings it would be a bleak and disturbing world if his power and presence were a matter of continual guesswork, and if we could never point with any certainty at something which lies within reach of our senses and say 'the finger of God is here'. The sacraments are not primitive rituals, magical practices through which we try to make God our servant, but the footprints that mark his passage through our daily life.

John F.X. Harriott, *The Empire of the Heart*

**PRAYER:**

Another irritable word! Another half-truth!
Another snide comment! Another impatience!
And so it goes on.
No matter how I try,
I'm always falling short of Christ's values,
his high ideals.
Why bother?
Most people I work with,
would laugh at me
if they knew that it does bother me.
And they seem to be happily
getting on with their lives without bothering!
So, Lord, should I care?
Yes, I've been baptised –
Yes, I committed myself to following you.
Yes, I know you love me and died for me.
And, yes again, I know we have your sacraments
to help us to keep on trying.

Let's make a deal, Lord.
I'll keep on bothering,
if you keep on helping me
to get up after each fall
to try again. Done?

## · 8 ·

# Meeting Christ at School

While visiting Jacopenny farm at Hullbridge, one half-term holiday, with my wife and a group of young children, I saw a collection of shepherds' crooks for sale. The farm is famous, locally, for its large and varied range of unusual animals and birds. It also has a simple tea shop, with a few mementoes for the children to buy. In a rack standing just inside the door there was, on this occasion, a selection of hand-carved walking sticks and shepherds' crooks. I took an immediate fancy to one of them and recognised its potential as a teaching aid at school. It has proved to be of great value. It comes into class with me when we are speaking about Christ, the Good Shepherd. Or with it I pretend to be a bishop, when we are studying his role in the diocese, and we are learning about the bishop's mitre and crosier. The crook is also a useful visual aid when we have a school or year assembly on the theme of 'Pastoral Care'.

Every school has a structure and system of providing pastoral care. Few who administer it realise the origin of the concept. It has its roots in the teaching of Jesus, that he is the Good Shepherd, who loves and cares for his sheep. The English word 'pastor', and naturally 'pastoral', comes from the Latin word 'pastor' meaning 'shepherd'. Hence the Latin for 'Good Shepherd' is *Pastor Bonus*. Therefore the natural symbol for every pastoral team in our schools is the shepherd's crook.

Outside of education most people equate 'teacher' with the delivery of a subject in the classroom, but in fact the great majority of teachers also have another demanding role; that of form tutor, or in the primary school, the class teacher. This caring role has become ever more demanding as the family has come under attack and is not the stabilising influence in the lives of the children and young people that it once was. This is sadly illustrated by a comment overheard recently in a primary school playground.

*First boy:* 'Is Mick with your mum now?'
*Second boy:* 'Yea.'
*First boy:* 'You'll like him. He was my dad last year!'

The important ethos of a Christian school has much to do with the quality of the pastoral care. This means the quality of the loving concern and care shown by all the staff, not just teachers, in a school community. The word 'community' is significant because where a very real effort is constantly being made to think of the school as a large Christian family and build it into a community, there you will find the caring and love of Christ in action.

In Britain today it is becoming more and more obvious that each of our Christian schools is proving to be a sanctuary or an oasis, where vulnerable children and young people can find respite, stability and security, if only for a few hours, in an increasingly malfunctioning society; a sanctuary where they are respected as unique human beings who have a divine purpose and presence within; an oasis where the environment provides and promotes values and standards that give a balanced and happy meaning to life.

For personal reasons one of my daughters transferred, for her A-level work, from a Catholic High School to a high profile, close to the top of the National league table, local Grammar school. She found the ethos of that school immediately different from what she had been accustomed to. Academic success was the one and only target. When my wife and I sat in front of one of her A-level teachers, at the first parents' evening, we were told, with a smile, that our daughter would pass (which she did the following year). I commented that the report we had received told us that she would achieve a C (pass marks at A-level range from A to E). The teacher replied that in their school they only counted A–Cs as passes. She continued, 'we don't really want anyone who achieves below a C. We make life really difficult in the first term, for the weaker students, so that they drop out!'

The first school mentioned above is renowned locally for the pastoral care of its students (and it does well academically). The second is renowned for competing with another Grammar school, in this conurbation, for the highest possible place on the National League tables. The cost is high for the weak, who 'go to the wall'. Many students from such schools may achieve wonderful results and gain a very lucrative career. They may really 'get on in life', but they have been robbed of the most important of all gifts, the love of Christ, experienced through the dedicated pastoral care of their teachers. However, we meet Christ in the school, not only in the important pastoral care but also in the quality of the teaching and learning.

At the time of Jesus, in the hill town of Nazareth, with its supposed population of two thousand, the boys would have gone to school from the ages of five to twelve, at the local synagogue. Scholars are in no doubt that Jesus could read and write (although there is no record of Jesus writing) both Aramaic, his native language, and Hebrew, as used in the synagogue. There would have been no pastoral care system in his school, for the rabbi and the *hazzan,* who worked in the synagogue, would have known the family life of Jesus well. And family life was strong in those times. Jesus reveals his education when he starts his ministry; reading in the synagogue and debating with the Jewish leaders.

Jesus, the teacher, is worthy of study. He taught with authority (Mk 21:27) and he was concerned with the truth. In fact he went further, declaring that he *was* the truth. 'I am the Way, the Truth and the Life' (Jn 14:6) John opens his Gospel declaring that Christ is full of the truth (1:1;14) In the course of his teaching, as recorded in John's Gospel, Jesus tells his audience twenty-five times that he is telling them the truth. That is surely what all teachers are concerned with; imparting the truth.

Whether pupils are having a lesson in science, maths, history, or they are in an RE class, they are being taught the truth. And Christ is the truth. Whether the teacher is a Christian, a Moslem, a Buddhist or an atheist, if they are doing their job correctly they are imparting the truth and Christ has told us that he is the truth.

Those of us who are teachers need frequently to remind ourselves of how close we are to Christ in the form room, as pastoral guides, and in the class room as subject teachers, imparting and helping our students to discover the truth. Those who are not in education need to remind themselves that education cannot be reduced to places on a league table. Also, that the Christian Church is involved in education for no other reason than it would be the direct wish of Christ; for in school pupils can experience the loving care of Christ and search for him who is *'the way, the truth and the life'*.

**READING:**

Jesus Christ has been given to us as our model and teacher. He came to teach us by word and example how greatly the Father deserves to be loved, and how he wills to be loved by people. It was not only in his own name that he loved, but in ours also. He fulfilled this primary and supreme obligation first of all for himself, and then for the whole human race, as its head and model. We can only acquit ourselves of this debt after him, and can only do so worthily through him, by making his dispositions our own, in so far as we are able to do so.

God's intention, therefore, was first that we should as Christians have a share in the treasury of divine knowledge and love that he bestowed on his only Son; then, that we should make the same use as Jesus of the knowledge that we have of God, and of the love that has been poured into our hearts by the Holy Spirit (Rom 5:5). This we do by consecrating ourselves to the Father as Jesus did, and imitating him by loving God with our whole mind, our whole heart and our whole strength. Lastly, in order that we may follow our Lord as closely as possible, we should recall how he was always thinking of his Father and how all his acts were traceable to the love he bore him.

John Nicholas Grou, *Meditations on the Love of God*

**PRAYER:**

Father, as your children,
each and everyone of us needs loving care.
And we do not doubt your immeasurable love
for each one of us.
Our own children, vulnerable and impressionable,
living in a malfunctioning society,
are in special need of loving pastoral care.

When at school may they receive that,
through the professional and dedicated
love and concern of their teachers.
And may parents and teachers be ever
united in making Christ and his love
a reality in their young lives.

## · 9 ·

# Meeting Christ while Decorating

Stripping wallpaper can be fun, if it comes off the wall in long strips. If it doesn't then it can really try your patience! Painting the ceiling can give you back and arm ache, while tiling can really test yourDIY skills. When, back in my long ago student years, I had a holiday job with professional builders and decorators, I learnt the importance of proper preparation for a decorating job. I had already learnt, from my grandfather, the importance of taking a pride in your work.

One of my most cherished childhood memories is of my grandfather working in his smithy. He was a wheelwright, a traditional craftsman, who was as skilled with the spokeshave as with the hammer and anvil. Between the ages of seven and nine I would slip into his smithy whenever I could, to watch him at work, sparks flying as he hammered out a red-hot iron. There would be a wonderful whoosh of water and steam as he plunged the glowing iron into a butt of water, alongside where he worked. Or I would find him in the woodwork shop delicately shaping a spoke for a wheel with his spokeshave. When a cart or wagon was painted and almost complete he would be there with his paint, brush and gold leaf, assuming the role of signwriter. I loved watching and being with him. He would say little as he concentrated on his work, just getting me to give him a hand by pumping the long arm of the bellows up and down, which made the forge fire glow when he needed it. Sometimes he would reward me with a threepenny piece.

It is only in recent years that I realised how multi-talented and skilful my grand father really was, especially as I believe that the traditional method of constructing a wooden wheel with iron rim has been all but lost. Now that I am at the age my grandfather was when I watched him, I wish I had been his apprentice and learnt the ancient art. How satisfying it must have been, to take rough blocks of wood and lengths of iron and from them, with the skills handed on from father to son, the strength of your arm, the judgement of your eye, and a few simple tools, to create a carriage or cart wheel. Strong, long-lasting, perfectly balanced, with shaped and decorated spokes.

In my tool box, that comes out when I'm decorating or doing household maintenance, I have some of my grandad's tools; they are simple and ancient in form. The mallet, the hammer, the cross-saw, the spokeshave, for example, have not changed for over two thousand years. Jesus, the craftsman, would certainly recognise them and would have possessed the skills to use them. Did he learn from Joseph how to make a cart wheel with an iron rim? One day he hung up those tools for the last time, looked round his plain workshop, and probably said to his mother, 'Sell the tools, they will bring in a little cash to keep you going.' He closed the rough door and left to become an itinerant preacher. I wonder who had Jesus' tools and what eventually became of them!

My wallpapering, and the tiling, are passable, but most definitely lack the professional touch. No one has, yet, passed any critical comment, but I am very well aware of the inadequacies; corners and joints that could have been more expertly finished. I have not and could not end up with a perfect job. Jesus, in his carpentry work, did not and could not make a perfect plough, door or wheel.

From the human point of view, it is not possible to make a perfect anything. The materials available for use are never perfect and our skills, which may be excellent, always lack something, as any honest craftsman will acknowledge. Perfection must always be the target, but it is not ultimately within our grasp. Only God can produce perfection. As a human being Jesus could not produce any perfect piece of joinery in his workshop. However he could work perfectly; and that he most definitely did.

To use the talents and skills God has given us, to the best of our ability, especially if they are in the service of others, is to give glory to God; it is to pray. Jesus most certainly would be praising his Father in this way. However there was a deeper meaning and direction to his work.

Christ, as the second person of the Trinity, lived constantly in love. While his gnarled and cut hands hammered and sawed, doing his work as well as he possibly could, he was in union with God, His Father. Every touch of his hands as he swung the hammer, every judgement his mind made, every breath, every heart beat, all were acts of love for his Father.

In his best-selling book, *Anam Cara. Spiritual Wisdom from the Celtic World,* John O'Donohue reminds us that 'the body is a sacrament'. The old familiar Catechism of yesteryear defined a sacrament as 'an outward sign of inward grace' or if you prefer, 'a visible sign of invisible grace'. The Apostle Paul, in his first letter to the Christians of Corinth (6:19) says 'do you not know that your body is a temple of the Holy Spirit, who is in you?' If the Holy Spirit is present in each one of us, how much more must that same Spirit be present in the temple of Christ's body! Every one of Christ's physical actions was a visible sign of his invisible love of the Father. His whole body, with every heart beat, every breath, every physical movement expressed outwardly the immeasurable love that dwelt within.

Our imperfect individual actions, are of some value as prayer, if offered to the Father; but they are transformed, and of immense value, if we offer them in union with Christ, the Son of God. The Father cannot refuse his Son's constant gift of love, made during his human life time, through the sacrament of his body. Now, ever living to make intercession for us, our actions can be offered to the Father through Christ's most glorious wounds.

When engaged in any activity, whether it is decorating, gardening, shopping or any of our daily occupations, we can be united with Christ. We can offer, with him, to the Father our love, from deep within us. Our 'temple' is not a static, inert thing, it is a sacrament which brings us to union, imperfect because of our imperfections, but into real union with the Father, in Christ. I only have to offer myself, at the start of the day, and try, as often as possible, to recall that offering through the day. To walk down the road aware that each step is an act of love, offered in union with Christ; sit quietly on the bus, breathe deeply and remind myself that each breath this day is an act of love. Each, and every day, we breathe 23,000 times. What an immense number of acts of love! How many times do our hearts beat? We can live, as we are called to, as Christ's disciples, in close union and harmony with the Holy Trinity. At the end of a day sanctified by the presence and assistance of the Holy Spirit; our offering of every thought, word and deed – including the involuntary natural acts of breathing, heart beats etc – can be offered to the Father through the glorious wounds of Christ. We can say to the Father, just before we sleep, there's another day of my life for you, offered in love.

**READING:**

Little things come daily, hourly, within our reach, and they are not less calculated to set forward our growth in holiness, than are the greater occasions which occur but rarely.

Moreover, fidelity in trifles, and an earnest seeking to please God in little matters, is a test of real devotion and love. Let your aim be to please our dear Lord perfectly in little things, and to attain a spirit of childlike simplicity and dependence. In proportion as self-love and self-confidence are weakened, and our will bowed to that of God, so will hindrances disappear, the internal troubles and contest which harassed the soul vanish, and it will be filled with peace and tranquillity.

John Nicholas Grou, *Manual for Interior Souls*

**PRAYER:**

> To love you, Lord, all day and every day.
> That's the target, and it's not easy!
> We are so busy; rushing here and there.
> Off to work, home again, out to the shops,
> washing, ironing, house cleaning –
> then slumped in front of the telly. Life is so full!
> Where's the time to pray?
>
> Lord, help us to understand
> that we don't have to stop anything we are doing,
> we haven't got to change our life style,
> (although all that rushing around can't be good for us)
> to give all our love to you.

We must first *want* to do it.
Then, with your help, we need to offer,
at the beginning of each day –
and during the day, if we can remember –
everything; every thought, word and deed,
to you as little gifts of love.
Each then becomes a prayer,
and we are praying all day long.
Lord, help us to *want* to try;
and bless our efforts with success.

## · 10 ·

## MEETING CHRIST IN THE DOLE QUEUE

Many years ago I found myself standing in the dole queue at the local Benefits Office. It was not an experience that I would care to repeat. I found myself there because the company that I had worked for – it is a complex story – sacked me! That result did not come suddenly, it was preceded by months of anxiety and distress (particularly for my wife), while the managing director of the company tried to make life so difficult for me that I would give up and go voluntarily. My tenacious character was not taken account of and I hung on, despite the constant daily harassment. In the end I was given my P60 and told to clear my desk. I took the case to a solicitor and the Industrial Tribunal was involved. The company settled out of court. But I still did not have a job!

According to modern scholars it is very probable that Jesus would have known periods of unemployment. It is unlikely that Jesus was the only *tekton* (that is best translated as 'woodworker') in the small town of Nazareth. Although it was an occupation demanding a wide range of skills, there would hardly be enough employment within his own community to keep him fully occupied and, more importantly, able to provide for his mother and himself. Some scholars have suggested that Jesus may well have found employment, for a while at least, in Sepphoris, a major city of Galilee that was only 3.7 miles to the north of Nazareth and just about an hour's walk away. Sepphoris had been destroyed during a revolt against Rome in 4BC. Herod Antipas, the ruler of Galilee, chose to have his capital at Sepphoris and it was being magnificently restored just at the time when Jesus would have been looking for employment.

Jesus certainly belonged to the poor, who had to work hard for their living, but he was not at the lowest rung of society. As a craftsman he would have been better off than the labourers and, at the very bottom of the social scale, the slaves, who were owned and worked almost to death by the big landowners. Poverty is a relative term and, by our standards, life at that time was very precarious, even for the middle classes, but definitely for men who lived by their inherited skills and crafts. Jesus would have been intimately acquainted with poverty. He had been born in someone else's stable; in his travels he had made the statement, 'the Son of Man has nowhere to lay his head' (Lk 9:58); and he was buried in someone else's tomb. There was, of course, no unemployment benefit in those days; if you did not work, you did not eat!

Despite the humorous portrayal of the dole queue in the popular film *The Full Monty*, it is not a fun place to be. My encounter was brief, but very memorable. The first emotion was one of shame; I remember looking round repeatedly to check that there was no one in that large office who would recognise me. I did not want my neighbours knowing and gossiping. There was also a bitter sense of rejection. I was convinced that I had done my best in my last job. I had made sacrifices for the company, taken on additional responsibilities and worked extra long hours. I had given loyal support to its proprietor, when there had been severe difficulties, but I had still been disposed of; and a new, younger man put in my place. It is bad enough being made redundant when trade and economic forces make a company 'down-size' and 'shed workers', but it is bitterly hard when loyal and faithful service is rewarded with a kick in the teeth! I should have remembered Jesus; but I didn't. His devotion to caring for the sick and helping all who turned to him was rewarded with the crowd's shout, 'crucify him', on his life's last day.

I *knew* I could get work, because I had certain skills, but I *felt* worthless. The responsibility of having a worrying wife at home and very young, dependent children increased the anxiety. I met myself in the dole queue; I did not meet Christ. At least, I did not recall and meditate upon Christ's presence, as I could have done. I felt too bitter, too angry; instead, as I recall, I just managed to keep praying, 'Please help me to find a job.' After a while – God never seems to work in a hurry – my prayer was answered.

With hindsight and the distance of time, it is possible to realise that Christ was with me all the time, as he is with everyone, in the Benefits office and the Job Seekers shop. Important as money is for the unemployed, especially the long-term unemployed, it is the sense of shame, of rejection, of worthlessness, that is de-humanising and debilitating. I had certain advantages over most of the other people in my dole queue; a good education and certain skills to offer. Those without work, who, through no fault of their own, had little of either to call upon, must have felt so much more hopeless and despondent. It is not poverty that destroys people, but their loss of a sense of personal worth, dignity and respect; and worst of all, hope. It's an old cliché, but still true: we all need to be needed.

Surely one of the greatest and best insights of the Church in the last thirty years is that God has, throughout the Bible, shown a preferential option for the poor. While he has no favourites, as St Paul reminds us (Gal 3:28), still the history of salvation reveals God's particular concern for the poor, who are unable to fend for themselves.

From Exodus' (22:25) injunction:

> Do not take advantage of a widow or an orphan. If you do and they cry out to me, I will certainly hear their cry.

to the prophets, like Ezekiel (21:26):

> The lowly will be exalted and the exalted will be brought low.

and Amos (8:4):

> Hear this, you who trample the needy and do away with the poor of the land.

to Luke's Gospel and the words of Christ's mother (1:53):

> He has filled the hungry with good things but has sent the rich away empty.

And Christ himself who says that he has come especially for the poor (Lk 4:18):

> The Spirit of the Lord is on me,
> because he has anointed me
> to preach good news to the poor.

and later (Lk 6:20-21):

> Blessed are the poor.
> for yours is the kingdom of God.

> Blessed are you who hunger now,
> for you will be satisfied.

The final book of the Bible has these words (Rev 2:8):

> These are the words of him who is the First and the Last,
> who died and came to life again.
> I know your afflictions and your poverty
> – yet you are rich!

Can there be any doubt of Christ's love for the poor and the preferential option that we as his friends and followers should show? How can we ever have far from our thoughts his words, in the parable of the Sheep and the Goats, about the final Judgement that we will each face (Mt 25:34-35):

> Come, you who are blessed by my Father; take your inheritance,
> prepared for you since the creation of the world.
> For I was hungry and you gave me something to eat,
> I was thirsty and you gave me something to drink...
> ...whatever you did for one of the least of these brothers of mine,
> you did for me.

**READING:**

The very poor can and do sometimes rise to heights of heroism in terrible conditions. But sometimes they behave quite otherwise and understandably turn bitter and vicious. Certainly the state of poverty cannot be commended without qualification as a sure road to sanctity. Voluntary poverty may purify the spirit; but involuntary poverty is a horse of a different colour and to equate the two is to turn an affliction into a charism. In practice its distressing consequence can be, like fearing and blaming them, to distance ourselves from the poor; to praise and patronise them instead of offering relief. Here too, in a subtler way, our own responsibility is diminished, and the poor are required to fend for themselves. The truth is that the poor are our responsibility, an individual and collective responsibility, and that alleviating poverty, with all its crippling effects on human development, a Christian duty. And if we find ourselves shying from it, it is useful to delve for reasons.

John F.X. Harriott, *The Empire of the Heart*

**PRAYER:**

I'm suffering from appeal fatigue, Lord.
Two more in the post today –
and they're both going in the bin unopened!
I must be on the mailing list of every charity in Britain.
I expect I'm exaggerating, but it certainly feels like it.
They all use the most distressing pictures they can find
and even try a little blackmail with free labels and pens!
What to do? Give a little to each charity that begs
or a large sum to one or two favourite charities?
I don't suppose it matters, as long as we remember
    your words,
that what we do for the poor, we do for you.
And try to be as generous as we can.
How better to repay, a little of your generosity to me.
How can I say that I love you and not love your poor?
Lord, again I'm asking for help –
to remember to pray for the poor,
not to succumb to appeal fatigue
and to be a bit more generous than I have been.

# · 11 ·

# MEETING CHRIST IN THE PARK

The noise of the distant traffic would intrude, if you turned your attention to it; but it is still and tranquil in the early morning park. The autumn sun slants eagerly through the dripping trees, while, in the distance, unleashed dogs bound about the green. I pull my coat around me as I halt my walk to sit upon a damp bench. Soon, on this Saturday morning, the boys will pour in with their white footballs. A little later, as the morning matures, the elderly will gently meander, to sit quietly and companionably upon similar benches to mine. Couples, intent upon themselves, will come and stroll arm in arm; while pushchair-pushing parents will aim for the busy swings and climbing frames close to the far fence.

Reflecting upon the scene, the hymn 'Morning has Broken' comes readily to mind, particularly the words, 'like the first morning'. The beauty of God's creation is all around. My theology tutor, while I was training in the 1970s to be a teacher, was a Mr McCabe and his constant theme was the centrality of creation. We were quite wrong, he repeatedly told us, to believe that creation was the act of God, which took place in the past; it is a constantly present act. Creation, as the work of God, is at the centre of all that presently is and will be. I'm not sure that, at the time, I quite understood him; but I have remembered enough to make me stop and think, and from time to time, meditate upon my place as a tiny creature in God's mighty work of creation.

To be aware of the presence of God, and the works of his creation, is to pray. One of the biggest mistakes that we make is to equate prayer solely with the repeating of formulas, the saying of prayers. It is understandable for as child I first learnt to pray by learning set formulas by heart. For many years, right into my early teens, I used to rattle off, with no awareness of the meaning of the words, the night prayer my mother taught me:

*Angel of God, my guardian dear,*
　*to whom God's love commits me here,*
*Ever this night be at my side to light and rule,*
　*to guard and guide.*

Like a magical incantation that prayer was recited every night of my early life; I know it was every night because I was fearful of missing it out. Then, in my teens, I learnt a little more about prayer and, at first, chose new prayer formulas and finally prayed spontaneously.

The old catechism, once called *The Penny Catechism*, gave a simple description of prayer: 'Prayer is the raising of the mind and heart to God'. Apparently this originates from a definition of St John Damascene, who wrote in the eighth century. One of the most inspiring exponents of prayer, St Thérèse of Lisieux, described prayer as follows: 'For me, prayer is a surge of the heart; it is a simple look turned towards heaven, it is a cry of recognition and of love, embracing both trial and joy.' The words 'simple look' remind us that prayer is the living relationship between the children of God and their Father.

While the ideal, in private prayer, should be to

express ourselves in our own thoughts, words or gestures, there will always be an important place for set prayers. After all, Jesus himself taught us the perfect prayer, the Lord's Prayer, the family prayer of all Christians. It contains all that prayer should encompass, Adoration; Contrition; Thanksgiving (including praise) and Supplication. Many Christians have grown up using the acronym, **ACTS**, which has helped them to remember that prayer embraces much more than just asking God for help. Besides our own words, there are the words of Scripture, pre-eminently the Psalms, that make excellent prayers.

In addition to public worship, where set prayers have their natural place, there are occasions, for example, when we are learning to pray, or in times of tiredness, sickness, grief or depression, when the desire and need to pray is not matched by the ability. Then the written or learned prayers of others, praying from a similar situation, are quite literally, a God-send. These can often be an ideal starting point, or rich source of meditation, at our prayer time, which leads us into our own spontaneous prayer. The words of Scripture can, of course, assist and guide in the same way. (Sr Josie, an Ursuline Sister of Brentwood, said on her deathbed, 'Well, I'm glad I prayed when I could, because now I can't.')

I hold in my hand a variegated leaf of green and yellow, from the evergreen bush growing beside where I am sitting in the park. I marvel at its pattern, and the thought that each leaf on that bush is uniquely different from every other leaf; even more wonderful is the thought that no two leaves, anywhere in the world, are the same! I find that an almost incredible thought. God only creates uniquely and individually.

As a creature, from the hand of my God, I am not

only a unique individual, I have a unique and individual relationship with my Creator. He, who asks me to call him 'Father', has a relationship with me that is distinctly different from his relationship with any other creature. We are each aware how individual we are. We are also at different and varying stages in our individual relationship with our Creator Father. That must mean that we are all at different stages in our prayer life. As in the parable of the Sower, we can observe simple examples of those different stages, by looking around the park.

What can we see? There are the boys on a patch of worn grass over by the swings. They are chasing one another, diving and tumbling. A friendly rough and tumble. Now they are up and kicking a ball to one another. Little is said; it is a physical relationship.

They are like the people who, with a faith in God, immerse themselves in lots of worthy activities for the good of others, but do not consciously relate what they are doing to prayer; they are like Martha of Bethany (see Lk 10:40).

There is the business man, striding purposefully through the park, using it as a short cut from one road to another. So caught up in his own anxieties and concerns that he neither notices the beauty of the morning, the glories of nature, nor any other person in the park. He, in 'Prayer Park', is like the person whose prayer is totally centred upon his own needs and worries; who never thinks to praise God or thank him. Prayer is just another tool for the furtherance of self.

Strolling in the park are the people who are out to enjoy the sunny morning; they smile and exchange greetings. These are polite and pleasant phrases, like, 'Good morning'. 'How are you?' While on the surface, they are well-intended, these exchanges are shallow and empty of any desire to be involved. It is relationship, without involvement and cost. Any sincere reply about the condition of your health or the welfare of your family, is likely to be experienced as threatening; and the conversation speedily ended.

Such people are like those who pray with rigid safe formulas, anxious to fulfil the duty to pray, but with no sense that prayer is an exchange in a loving and caring relationship. There is no risking a really committed relationship with God; just in case he should ask something of them.

Oblivious to the beauties of nature and everyone else in the park, the young couple sit on a bench wrapped up in themselves. Early in love they want to find out all about 'the other'. Love blinds them to all else. In 'Prayer Park' the couple are like those who have just discovered that 'God is Love' (1 Jn 4:16) and enjoy the warm experience of *knowing*, perhaps for the first time, how deeply they are loved by God. For them the words of St John, 'whoever lives in love, lives in God, and God in him' (1 Jn 4:17) have become very real. Prayer for such a Christian is awareness that 'nothing can separate us from the love of Christ' (Rom 8:35) and that it is Christ who lives within (Gal 2:20). All actions, thoughts, words become prayers, not to a God up in the skies but to Christ who dwells within. Such a Christian is like Mary of Bethany (Lk 10:39) who is close to Christ, but whose faith and perseverance is yet to be tested. Mary, in her Bethany home, still had to pass through the testing experience of the death and resurrection of Christ.

An elderly couple, content in one another's presence, mature in living and loving, sit meditatively on a far park bench. They hold hands and, without exchanging a word, gaze contentedly upon the boys playing football; the mothers pushing their buggies; the business man taking a short cut through the park; and the young couple. There is no need for words, they are contentedly together; they simply savour each moment, each 'picture' before them, aware that *life* and *love* are all. In 'Prayer Park' the elderly couple are like those who have persevered in faith and have matured in the love of God; 'prayer' for them is the very direction of their lives and their love. They are aware that they live continually in the presence of God, who is love, and everything in their lives is united with Christ and offered with him and through him to the Father. Yes, they use, from time to time, set prayers and they meditate, but it is life itself, with their constant love, which has become prayer. Christ prays to the Father in them. For them, prayer really is the raising of the mind and heart to God.


**READING:**

It is by frequent raising of my mind and heart to God, as to their proper object, that the practice of the presence of God becomes easy, and that the love of God increases and is strengthened in my soul. Then will I realise what St Augustine meant when he said: 'God is closer to us than we are to ourselves', and, 'I sought you outside of me, and all the while you were within me' (*Confessions*).

And this way of loving God, the loveliest and easiest of all, is at the same time also the most efficacious, because it need never be interrupted. There is nothing to prevent my mind and my heart being raised to God, and what we do often cannot fail, in time, to produce a noticeable effect. Moreover, the more one thinks of God, the more loveable he becomes; and the more one loves, the more one wants to love. Thus the practice of the presence of God, being an exercise of love, is bound to result in an increase of love.

John Nicholas Grou, *Meditations on the Love of God.*

**PRAYER:**

    How do I pray about prayer, Lord?
    I can ask you to make my faith stronger;
        – that would improve how I pray.
    Please strengthen my faith.
    I can ask for much more trust in you,
        – then I would not doubt that you love me,
    and hear and answer my prayers.
    Please increase my trust.
    I can ask you to deepen my love,
    for you, and for those around me;
        – that would help me to be more generous
    in giving time to prayer, and I'd appreciate you more.
    That could lead me to be continually thankful.
    Lord, please deepen my love.

    One of my friends prays for the gift of tongues;
    if you don't mind, Lord,
    I'd prefer to pray for the gift of wisdom.
    Then I wouldn't do such stupid things, some times;
    and I would be able to help and advise others.
    That leaves me to ask for an increase in hope.
    Actually this whole prayer is built upon hope,
    because if you had not given me some hope,
    I would not have had the courage to badger you
    about faith, trust, love and wisdom!

## · 12 ·

## MEETING CHRIST IN THE SURGERY

Looking round the surgery waiting room, at the posters warning of the dangers of smoking and instructions on how to detect breast cancer, I wondered why the other eleven people were there. One or two of them I knew and we had already exchanged nods and greetings, deliberately avoiding the usual question, 'How are you?' for fear of an honest answer on this occasion. I knew that I looked well and they must have wondered what I was doing there. It was actually a minor, but irritating ailment, not observable to the human eye.

This waiting room must have seen some tragedies; I knew of a few. Sarah, my wife's friend, who came here in a terrible state of despair after being delivered, at home, of a still-born child. Jim, a neighbour, who sat here and learnt in the consulting rooms that his cancer was inoperable and he had only a few months left. Tim, a twelve-year-old, who was rushed here then immediately off to hospital and died two days later of meningitis. And while there were doubtless other tragic stories, what of the many people who sat here and received wonderful healing help and good news, when they had feared the worst? Healing the sick: what a wonderful calling. We hear so much about the faults and failings of our National Health Service and so little about the dedication and healing skills of our doctors and nurses.

Like poverty, at the time of Jesus bad health was viewed through the eyes of religion. Both were believed to be signs of God's disfavour, punishment for sin. 'As he went along, Jesus saw a man blind from birth. His disciples asked him, "Rabbi, who sinned, this man or his parents, that he was born blind?"' The disciples were speaking, asking a genuine question, from a position of received wisdom; they had grown up in a society that linked blindness, disease (like leprosy) and all illness with sin. 'Neither this man nor his parents sinned', said Jesus. There is no direct link or connection between ill health and sin.

The disciples' misconception is still with us. When misfortune strikes or ill health comes, occasionally you still hear people say, 'What have I done to deserve this?' 'Why has God done this to me?' Disease and death is not of God's making. Both science and religion can shed some light upon this problem.

Biologists tell us that the human body has evolved over a period of millions of years. Our Creator, God, could have created in any way he wished, but science reveals to us that God actually started and guided the process over a vast period of time. Humans have evolved, and are still evolving, which means that physically I am what has been passed on to me. Not just the genes that determine the colour of my eyes, my height and my intelligence but also the genes which carry a disability, like defective eye sight, and, more seriously, disease.

'If this world is good and the creation of God, how is it that there is evil around and sickness and death?' That question has been with the human race from its very earliest beginnings. It is the question that the second and third chapters of the Book of

Genesis tries, in a religious way, to answer. We were created to be free, happy and healthy; but our first parents failed a simple test of obedience. They sinned. As a result, freedom was lost (we have to work); pain came in (childbirth would be painful). Still we misuse our free will. People are told of the danger to their health from smoking, but still they smoke. Excessive alcohol, drugs and so on, can all bring illness and suffering.

Recently I was told that Emily Brooking, a thirty-two-year-old mother of two little girls, aged six and four, had died. She had lived in an attractive detached house in a prosperous neighbourhood and her husband worked in a bank in the city of London. She had been ill for over a year with lung cancer. 'How can there be a God', the female friend of Emily remarked to me. 'How can a God be so cruel as to take a young mother and leave her husband with two little girls to bring up on his own. Where's the justice in that?' Julie was too emotional to want to listen to me; but I did have an explanation, a true story, for her. One day perhaps I will have an opportunity to tell her.

I had known Emily from years before when she was Emily Smythe, a fourteen-year-old pupil at Sandown Court School at Tunbridge Wells, Kent. That was the first school in which I taught, and Emily was in my form. She was a pretty girl, but precocious and headstrong. One day we were having a lesson which involved a discussion on the dangers of smoking. Emily was loud in proclaiming to the class, with pride, that she smoked and saw nothing wrong in it. She told everyone to take no notice, it was just teachers and parents trying to stop kids having fun with scary stories. Everyone does it, she declared.

As it happened, the following Saturday I was out shopping with my wife, when we turned a corner to come upon Emily, with two of her friends, with cigarettes in their hands. Emily was closest to me. She said, 'Hello, Sir', stepped closer and deliberately puffed cigarette smoke into my face. All the girls laughed, turned and walked off. My wife was disgusted and asked. 'Aren't you going to do anything?' I told her that I would deal with it at school. But I was inexperienced and didn't.

Some months later Emily's family moved away from Tunbridge Wells and I did not see her or hear of her again for fifteen years. Then one day, I was sitting in the waiting area of the local opticians, when the attractive young woman opposite said to me, 'The receptionist called you Mr Castle. You used to teach in Tunbridge Wells, did you?' It turned out to be Emily, now married, living in the area and with two young children. I made no comment but I noticed that she was still smoking. The next time I heard of her she was in hospital. Eventually I heard the sad news that she had died. God cannot be blamed for our misuse of free will.

How did Jesus cope with his own pain and suffering? Did he treat it with indifference or stoically welcome it? No, he tried to escape it. In the Garden of Gethsemane (Mk 14:36) he pleaded with his Father that he might be spared the pain and suffering that he knew was coming. 'Abba, Father,' he said, 'everything is possible for you. Take this cup [of suffering] from me.'

Luke in his Gospel adds that he prayed so earnestly that 'his sweat was like drops of blood' (Lk 22:44). It is clear that Jesus, like any human, did not want to suffer, and that pain was not just physical but also psychological torture; rejection, abandonment and total humiliation.

When Jesus is convinced that his Father wants him to accept it, his prayer changes. 'Yet not what I want, but what you want' (Mk 14:36). There is our model. We are right to do everything, morally and reasonably possible, to avoid pain and suffering, and to pray hard to our Father that it might be taken away. But the point may come when we need to change our prayer to one of acceptance, laying ourselves with trust in his loving hands.

Fr Eddie Fitzgerald SDB wrote the following when he was very seriously ill from cancer (he died a few months later):

> 'The reality is that once we begin to accept our situation, without wallowing in it, without giving in to it, our perspective subtly begins to change. St Irenaeus was right: "What has not been accepted cannot be redeemed." Serious illness can make us look at our life from an altogether more radical viewpoint. It can force us to do things and change things we wouldn't do or change given other circumstances.'

Trust must follow acceptance:

> 'What illness and suffering do is offer us a pathway strewn with unexpected twists and turns, so much so that we cannot presume to know what will happen next. It forces us to put our trust in Someone greater than ourselves. As Isaac Bashevis Singer put it: "Life is God's great novel. Let him write it."'

The faith and trust that Jesus placed in his Father was rewarded on the third day, when God raised him to life (Acts 2:32). If we can only bring ourselves to that point, with Christ, of trusting and accepting what cannot be changed, the Father will raise us up.

> 'Now if we are children, then we are heirs – heirs of God and co-heirs with Christ, if indeed we share in his sufferings in order that we may also share in his glory' (Rom 8:17).

Belonging to Christ's community, his family of friends and followers, can also help; when someone we love is ill or we ourselves are engulfed in suffering there is the very real support of the community's love and prayers.

**READING:**

There are many different kinds of solitude. There is the solitude of suffering when you go through darkness that is lonely, intense and terrible. Words become powerless to express pain; what others hear from your words is so distant and different from what you are actually suffering. Everyone goes through that bleak time. Folk-consciousness always recognises that, at such a time, you must be exceedingly gentle with yourself. I love the image of the field of corn in autumn. When the wind catches the corn, it does not stand stiff and direct against the force of the wind; were it to do this, the wind would rip it asunder. No. The corn weaves with the wind, it bends low. And when the wind is gone, it weaves back and finds its own poise and balance again.

John O'Donohue, *Anam Cara*

**PRAYER:**

> Father, from the beginning of human time
> we have grappled with pain and suffering.
> Whatever is said, it still remains a mystery.
> We know you do not want your children
> to suffer – but we do!

You asked your Son, your dear and only Son,
to accept hideous suffering, and he did;
but not before he pleaded to be spared.
Spare us, we pray, from all pain and suffering;
but if there is no other way, help us to accept
and offer it to you, as Christ did.
You received his offering, and raised him up.
Receive us, all of us,
all our joys and all our sorrows,
that we might become like
to your own dear Son, now in glory.

## · 13 ·

# MEETING CHRIST AT DEATH

He heard! I'm now convinced that he heard. The single tear running down his right cheek was a response to my stumbling words. His last dying act, just minutes before the last breath.

I had sat with my father from 3.30 a.m., when the hospital chaplain came into the ward at Buckland Hospital, to anoint him, until this precious moment, just before midday. My brother, Peter, and I had responded to a call at 3 a.m. from the hospital and had gone immediately, because the telephone message was expected. The priest arrived soon afterwards. We all prayed together, and Peter and I received Holy Communion with Dad. His administrations completed, the priest left us to our vigil. This was not the first, but we could see that it was the most serious. At 7.30 a.m., as there was no apparent change in Dad's condition, my brother left to go to work.

Propped up in bed, my father drifted in and out of consciousness for the next few hours. Sitting on his right side, and facing him, I could easily hold his right hand, or stroke his arm, with my right hand. At about 10 o'clock he was conscious and it was then that I thought I noticed the first change. On a type of table that straddled the end of the bed, so directly in my father's line of vision, was an attractive flowering plant. I had my hand on his arm, and to make conversation I commented on the beauty of the flowers. Staring directly ahead at them he replied, 'They're lovely.' I suddenly suspected that he could not actually see them, so I raised my right hand to sweep it before his eyes. There was no reaction. Dad's sight had gone; and those words were actually his last. I was now convinced that the end was near and started saying little prayers into his right ear. At first I did not cope very well; I was feeling a numbness and I stumbled on the prayers. I knew dozens, but could not, at first, think of one! I could only think of repeating slowly, phrase by phrase, the Lord's Prayer and then the Hail Mary. I knew that there were other suitable prayers, but I just couldn't recall them. With pauses I continued and other short prayers and words started to come to me.

All feeling left his feet – a doctor came and checked – and then it departed his hands; and I was aware of that. He was peaceful and appeared to be in no pain; his body was simply closing down. I sent a message to my brother.

I had heard it said that hearing is the last sense to go, so, in that hope, I continued, every little while, to say short prayers directly into his ear. There was no visible indication that he heard me, and I began to have doubts. Then, after another Hail Mary, I said, 'You've been a wonderful Dad. We owe so much to you; you know we all love you.' I paused, feeling a little awkward and foolish, and then I saw it. A tear left the corner of his right eye and ran down his cheek. I sat there speechless, feeling tears welling up behind my eyes – then there was a disturbance and my brother arrived at the bedside with Anne, his wife, and Mark, my nephew. I went round the bed to report the situation. We sat round and I said a few more prayers into Dad's ear; but there was no further response. He gently stopped breathing fifteen minutes later.

Since my father's death I have often quietly and secretly wondered whether my father had really heard me: perhaps I just wanted to believe that he heard my words and the tear was unconnected. Then very recently I read of the first-hand experience of Bernadette Quinn (*Spirituality*, Dec '99). She was in hospital and at death's door; she could hear the nurse saying 'I can't get a pulse' and the doctor answering 'Neither can I!' Bernadette writes 'I wanted to shout out, "I can hear you!" but those glued lips could not be forced open, those heavy eyelids could not be lifted.'

> 'Later I heard a priest praying over me and I was certain those moments with the priest would be my last moments before death, but the thought did not frighten me. What was terrible was the awful loneliness I felt setting out on my own on the journey from life and the husband I loved, to the next life.
>
> What I wanted more than anything else then was my husband beside me; to hear comforting words and prayers from the priest. The latter, perhaps, thinking that I couldn't hear, didn't delay. If he had only known how much I longed for him to stay until I was brought to the operating theatre.'
>
> 'Three Times at Death's Door' *Spirituality, Dec '99*

What Bernadette wanted was to have the closeness of a loved one and 'to hear comforting words and prayers'. That was so reassuring to learn. The presence of the loved one must be, to the dying person, the presence of Christ himself at the bedside, for Christ dwells by faith in the hearts of his disciples (Eph 3:17).

There appears to be a tendency, in all types of health care, in our times, to treat the human body as a machine. Doctors and nurses genuinely do all they can to repair it, but they appear to lose interest if it transpires that that is not possible. For Christians the body is precious, the very temple of the Holy Spirit. St Paul is very insistent upon the dignity of the human body in his first letter to the Christians of Corinth, who have been involved in some very dubious practices. 'Do you not know that your body is a temple of the Holy Spirit, who is in you, whom you have received from God?' (1 Cor 6:9).

How best can we prepare for the moment of death? What would we do if we learnt that we are to die in a few hours? Rush off to the church to pray or seek out a priest for the sacraments?

There are two traditional Christian stories, both with the same message: St Francis of Assisi, who was hoeing his garden, was asked what he would do if he suddenly learnt that he was to die at sunset that day. He said, 'I would finish hoeing my garden!' A story is told of Martin Luther: One morning, while discussing points of theology with a group of friends, he was asked 'What would you do, if you knew for sure that the Lord was coming tonight?' In his usual quick and impetuous manner, Luther replied, 'I'd go out into my garden and plant an apple tree', meaning he would go about his ordinary business.

In other words, if we are daily trying to live a life of union with Christ, and we are offering our whole day to the Father, through him, as prayer, then we are ready. Nothing more is needed. There is no special 'holy' act necessary, for all our actions are sacred if lived in union with Christ, our lover.

There is a more modern, more light-hearted story, on the same theme: It was time for the traditional Christmas Midnight Mass and the ushers were trying to find places for the latecomers. George, an elderly usher who had seen many Midnight Masses, spotted a gentleman of about the same age standing just inside the door. He approached and recognised the man. 'Good evening', he said, 'don't you come every year at this time?' 'Yes' smiled the visitor. 'Why don't you come more often?', George asked. 'Well' the gentleman replied, 'I like to let the Lord get a glimpse of me once a year, so that he won't ask who I am when the time comes!' The following lines sum up the story:

> Each time I pass an open church
> I think I'll pay a visit,
> So when at last I'm carried in,
> The Lord won't say, 'Who is it?'

Our meeting with Christ, at the moment of death, will not be the meeting of two strangers, if day by day we persevere in trying to live our daily lives in union with him.

**READING:**

If Christ were to come at this moment, would he find faith on the earth – in us ? Where is our faith? What are the proofs of it? Do we believe that this life is only a short passage to a better one? Do we believe that we must suffer with Jesus before we can reign with him? Do we look upon the world as a vain show, and death as the entrance into true happiness? Do we live by faith? Does it animate us? Do we enjoy the eternal truths that it presents to us? Do we feed our souls with them, as we nourish our bodies with food?

May we not fear that the kingdom of heaven will be taken from us and given to others who will bring forth more fruit. This kingdom of heaven is faith, when it swells and reigns in the heart. Blessed are the eyes that see this kingdom; flesh and blood have not seen it; earthly wisdom is blind to it. To realise its glories, we must be born again, and to do this we must die to self.

      Francois Fenelon, *'Selections From Fenelon'*

**PRAYER:**

>Loving Father, is it morbid to think about my death?
>Most of my friends would say 'yes', leave it alone.
>It must surely be important though,
>because then the 'forever' will be decided.
>Then I'll find out if I'm going
>to be with Love, with You,
>who I've desired to be with, all my life;
>or whether my loving, of you and others,
>has not been up to scratch
>and I will be separated from Love.
>Temporarily or permanently?
>How tough is that judgement going to be?
>I'm not going to ask you any questions
>about how, or when,
>because I know you won't tell me.
>I only ask that you will help me,
>today, and everyday, to live more lovingly.
>Then I may be ready when you call.

## · 14 ·

## MEETING CHRIST AT THE WAR MEMORIAL

As I stood in the small crowd around the local war memorial, on Remembrance Day, waiting for the service to begin, I thought of Sergeant Finch. My reminiscing took me back to the 1950s and my boarding school days. For five years, on a Wednesday afternoon, for one hour, we had PT (not your modern PE) in all weathers. Just over ninety of us were arranged in ranks, in our singlets, shorts and plimsoles, out on the 'bounds' (this was a large tarmacked area, rather like a playground). The college had no gym so our PT took place *every* Wednesday of term time, no matter what the weather, rain or shine, frost or snow, out in the fresh air.

Sergeant Finch would arrive on his bike, in full khaki uniform, proudly wearing the crossed swords badge of an Army PT instructor of the First World War. At 1.55 p.m. we gathered for a prompt 2 p.m. start. He had been wounded at the first Battle of the Somme (1 July–19 November 1916) in which the staggering figure of 1,030,000 young men died. He had been repatriated to England, where, after he had recovered, he spent the rest of the War training and preparing young recruits for the Front. In the mid 1950s he must have been about sixty years of age but he had retained the erect posture and trim appearance of a very fit man.

Sergeant Finch treated us as though we were a new company of recruits. We had to stand in ranks, space out and number off, stand to attention or at ease, according to his order. He taught us according to the principles of Swedish drill, which was apparently the method used by the British Army at the time of the First World War. After fifteen minutes or so of energetic exercises, he would order, 'Stand at ease.' Legs apart and hands behind our backs, we would wordlessly obey. Then, no matter whether it was raining hard, snowing or blowing a gale, he would inform us that it was time to 'cool off'. Internally we groaned! This was the signal for yet another story from the trenches. At first it was interesting, but as the years passed and the repetitions grew, it became a little boring! However, I became very knowledgeable about the horrors of trench warfare; the stench of the deep mud, which seemed to have been everywhere; the rats that would snuggle up close to you at night, for your body heat; the soldiers who faked accidents to injure themselves and so avoid the horrendous conditions of the trenches; the whistle at dawn that summoned you to fix bayonets and 'go over the top' to face the machine gun fire and the wire.

Yes, in retrospect, I am grateful to Sergeant Finch, who brought home to me the amazing courage and heroism of the soldiers of the First World War; that brings me back, year after year, to stand and remember them at the local war memorial.

To continue with the service at the war memorial. After the silence and the trumpet call of the Last Post, the stirring words of Laurence Binyon are read:

> They shall not grow old as we that are left
>   grow old;
> Age shall not weary them nor the years
>   condemn.
> At the going down of the sun and in
>   the morning
> We will remember them.

Those words were written of the dead of the First World War. That finished well over eighty years ago! No one standing with me at that war memorial would be old enough to remember any soldier, sailor or airman who died in that War. You can only remember someone that you have known. I can clearly remember Sergeant Finch, but that was from the 1950s, not the 1910s. And he died a natural death. There are a small number standing with me who knew and can remember someone, a father, brother or an uncle perhaps, who died in the Second World War, but their numbers are gradually dwindling.

It is true that nowadays we recall not only the dead of the two World Wars but also all those who have died in wars throughout the twentieth century; one hundred million of them, from the Boer War to the Gulf War. However, the great majority of our population have no memory of anyone who has died in warfare. Not one of the many teenagers that I teach has any memory of anyone, military or civilian, who has died as a result of warfare. How can we solemnly say then, 'we will remember them'?

Some years ago I was commissioned by a well-known Christian publishing house to compile a large collection of prayers. After the manuscript had been submitted and accepted, the editor rang me to ask if I minded very much if they took out the section which was headed, 'Prayers for the Dead'.

He explained that their Protestant book outlets would not accept the book if the section remained in it. I reluctantly agreed.

On Remembrance Day we touch upon one of the unspoken differences between the Protestant and the Catholic traditions. Standing at the war memorial I am praying that all those who have died in armed conflict will receive and enjoy eternal happiness and peace with Christ; my friends from the local Protestant churches are 'remembering' them and thanking God for that memory.

The Remembrance Day service, at least in our village, makes much of the Armistice, ending the First World War, at the eleventh hour on the eleventh day of the eleventh month of the year. When, one year, I was asked to speak, I pointed out the incompleteness of this timing. If something happens at the eleventh hour it is almost too late; there is a lack of completeness, for we think of the twelfth hour as complete; midday or midnight. The Armistice was threefold in its incompleteness. It did not bring the lasting peace that all desired, as the following, equally dreadful, Second World War proved. The eleventh hour, day and month leave us with a challenge. Remembrance Day is not just a passive remembering, but also an active challenge to work for a peace that will last; the peace of Christ.

St Paul, writing to the Christians of Colosse, referring to the suffering of Christ, wrote:

> 'Now I rejoice in what was suffered for you, and I fill up in my flesh what is still lacking in regard to Christ's afflictions, for the sake of his body, which is the church. I have become its servant by the commission God gave me to present to you

the word of God in its fullness – the mystery that has been kept hidden for ages and generations, but is now disclosed to the saints. To them God has chosen to make known among the Gentiles the glorious riches of this mystery, which is Christ in you, the hope of glory' (Col 1:24-27).

Nothing is lacking from the saving death and resurrection of Christ; it cannot be, as it was the total gift of himself to the Father, made in complete obedience and love. Equally the peace of Christ cannot be improved upon. However, if sacrifices are not made to proclaim, as Paul did so generously, the Good News of Christ's sacrifice, then there is a lacking, for we need to know about, accept and co-operate with Christ's saving act. Once that has happened we are caught up in a wonderful mystery – Christ is within us.

A young teenage friend of my family, Julia, made a small banner for Remembrance Day for her school design and technology coursework. It was beautifully executed and showed an attractive bunch of poppies, and underneath the caption, *Lest we forget*. For modern young people that must be the direction that 11 November takes. They cannot 'remember', nor should they be expected to; but they should learn about and be encouraged not to forget the sacrifices made by many millions of people, to secure the present and the future for them.

The war memorial stands in a prominent place outside the village church of St Nicholas. It carries line after line of names; from both World Wars. Christ stands with us there. 'Where two or three come together in my name, there am I with them' (Matthew 18; 20). These were his brothers and sisters, who died brutally, as he did. If, like Christ, they generously went to their deaths in a spirit of sacrifice, then they must be particularly dear to him. As weekly we recall Christ's sacrifice, so annually we must remember to recall theirs.

**READING:**

Be fixed and unshaken in your faith; care for each other with a brother's love and make common cause for the truth. Give way to one another in the Lord's own spirit of courtesy, treating no one as inferior. When it is in your power to do a kindness, never put it off to another time, for charity is death's reprieve.

St Polycarp (died c.155) *'Letter to the Philippians'*

**PRAYER:**

> To stand in Flanders Fields,
> in those vast cemeteries,
> with their endless lines of white crosses –
> young men in their teens and early twenties.
> That's an experience, Lord, that everyone should have.
> Especially the leaders of the nations,
> who still send young people to war.
> The Gulf War, the Falklands War –
> on top of all the other wars of the twentieth century;
> how many more dead are we going
> to stand and remember,
> each November of the twenty-first century?
> Lord of the war-dead,
> grant them everlasting peace with you,
> and lasting peace for us.

# · 15 ·

# MEETING CHRIST AT THE PARTY

It was a surprise birthday party, to celebrate the half century of Graham, a family friend. As he approached the Yacht Club, where he thought he had a booking as a saxophonist for the evening, we were all hushed to silence, as we waited, almost breathless, in the darkened club room. The full lights went on as Graham entered and over seventy voices shouted 'Happy Birthday'. It was as well that he did not suffer from a weak heart because the surprise was complete, and the astonishment genuine to everyone's delight. There were more delights to come, especially when Graham's parents, who should have been at home in Carlisle, walked in soon after.

The lights were dimmed, the bar area was well peopled, and not a few male eyes were caught by the beautiful young woman singer, who led the four piece band, when I recognised the presence of Christ. He came to mind because I had been meditating that morning on where Christ is to be found. In that club room unselfish goodness was all around me in the intentions and actions of Graham's family and friends. Christ cannot be separated from God; wherever the Father is, there is the Son and the Holy Spirit. When genuine goodness is evident, God is unmistakably present.

'On the third day a wedding took place at Cana in Galilee. Jesus' mother was there, and Jesus and his disciples had also been invited to the wedding' (Jn 2:1ff).

A few years ago, while in the Holy Land, my wife and I renewed our marriage vows at the small church in Cana, along with five other couples of our pilgrimage group. Scholars, however, doubt that the Cana shown to the modern pilgrim and tourist is genuinely the original place. Not that it matters very much, for the value is not in visiting heaps of ancient stones, but in recalling Christ's action and associating ourselves with that action.

In first-century Palestine marriages were arranged – it was marriage first and love afterwards. Apart from a blessing that was pronounced over the couple, the wedding was essentially a non-religious event and the rabbi was not expected to be in attendance. The ceremony was centred upon a legal contract, proposed and accepted. There was lots of dressing up; the bride and groom looked like and acted like a king and a queen, and much eating and drinking took place at the wedding banquet. The festivities began with a procession, in which the bridegroom's friends brought the bride to the groom's house. There a simple ceremony took place, followed by a wedding supper. Usually the festivities continued for seven days. The Mishnah (an authoritative collection of Jewish laws) ordained that the wedding of a virgin should take place on a Wednesday. Jesus probably arrived at Cana on Tuesday evening or Wednesday morning. Tradition has it that Mary, the mother of Jesus, who is mentioned first in the story, was the aunt of the bridegroom. That would explain how Jesus came to be invited and Mary's concern for the embarrassment of the young bridegroom when the wine ran out.

I once heard a preacher suggest (I do not know on what authority) that the wine ran out at the festivities because Jesus turned up with so many friends: a crowd of thirsty fishermen! Perhaps to persuade her son to attend the family gathering Mary had said, 'Do come; and bring your friends' (meaning two or three) and Jesus arrived with twelve!

I can remember my father coming home, grubby and tired from his daily work as a motor mechanic, to be greeted by the reminder from my mother that they were going out that evening. He grumbled. He grumbled as he ate his dinner and he grumbled as he changed to go out; and my mother took no notice! She knew something that Dad would always take care to forget; he always returned having enjoyed himself. I can now recognise the same reluctance in myself. Sometimes my wife reminds me of an evening social event and my first reaction is to grumble, because I don't want to go out having just arrived home from work. But invariably I return home happy to have made the effort, the water of my discontent transformed into the wine of contentment!

It was true of the day of the surprise fiftieth birthday party. I went with some reluctance, but when I started to see and reflect upon the goodness of so many people, I changed my tune. A real reluctance became a sense of privilege to witness and be a small part of the love shown to a friend. I was little more than an observer, but I saw such unselfishness. Seventy people wanted to contribute to the surprise and made a big effort to get to the club on time; they all brought presents(also a surprise for Graham); several women had contributed to and worked hard all afternoon to prepare the food; the band were offering their services without charge; a couple had given secret hospitality to Graham's parents until the moment arrived for them to appear at the party. And so it went on. All ordinary and, in themselves, unremarkable actions but all charged with love and the presence of Christ.

The water of the ordinary can be changed into wine by the simple realisation and recognition of what we see and are part of. Love was palpably present at Graham's party as it was in the love and concern shown by Mary and Jesus at the wedding at Cana. Christ's presence is never going to be recognised unless people open their eyes. Almost in desperation John the Evangelist says:

> 'Even after Jesus had done all these miraculous signs in their presence, they still would not believe in him' (Jn 12:37).

John goes on to quote the Prophet Isaiah;

> 'He has blinded their eyes
> and deadened their hearts,
> so they neither see with their eyes,
> nor understand with their hearts,
> nor turn – and I would heal them (Is 6:10).

That is all we have to do: open our eyes. Then the water of the ordinary will be transformed into the wine of the special. Is it not interesting that at the first recorded meal of Jesus with his friends he changed water into wine, and at his last meal he changed wine into his blood?

**READING:**

Prayer is the act and presence of sending this light from the bountifulness of your love to other people to heal, free and bless them. When there is love in your life, you should share it spiritually with those who are pushed to the very edge of life. There is a lovely idea in the Celtic tradition that if you send out goodness from yourself, or if you share that which is happy or good within you, it will all come back to you multiplied 10,000 times. In the kingdom of love there is no competition; there is no possessiveness or control. The more love you give away, the more love you will have. One remembers here Dante's notion that the secret rhythm of the universe is the rhythm of love which moves the stars and the planets.

John O'Donohue, *Anam Cara*

**PRAYER:**

>Lord, you recognised the importance
>of being with people, wherever they were.
>You were such a lively partygoer,
>that you got a reputation for often
>eating and drinking with sinners!
>Your goodness must have been a great attraction;
>And you saw the good present in
>those with the worst reputations in the neighbourhood.
>Lord, with your help I could be more positive
>and less judgemental about people.
>Please help me to recognise the goodness
>and generosity in the people around me.
>Not to be so free and easy with criticism,
>and so slow to see you
>in their goodness and generosity.
>Lord, open my eyes that I may see.

## · 16 ·

## MEETING CHRIST AT THE COFFEE MORNING

One of the proudest moments in the life of our extended family was the evening in 1983, when the Archbishop of Southwark, Michael Bowen, presented my mother, in the name of Pope John Paul II, with the *Bene Merenti* papal medal. She did not receive it for founding or leading a women's group, or writing articles and books, getting up in public to speak, or anything that involved being in the public eye. She was awarded this papal honour for an unbroken forty-five years of cleaning the church each week, polishing the brass, and making coffee for people after the Sunday morning Mass. The citation hangs on our wall at home and the medal is in a small showcase in St Paul's church, Dover, where she worshipped.

I have seen and helped her when, with no word of complaint, she has gone round the parish hall, after the Sunday coffee morning, collecting up the used cups and saucers for washing and putting away. Earlier I had observed the parishioners pour in, after the last morning service, collect a cup of coffee and a biscuit, then sit or stand deep in conversation, put down the dirty cups and walk out. It was always assumed that their coffee would be ready for them when they entered the hall and someone would clear up after them! My wife often speaks of the same assumption at two of the Mother and Toddler clubs that she helps with. She and a friend, generous volunteers, open the hall and put out the children's toys. They are making the coffee as the young mothers arrive with their toddlers. Deep in exchanging the local news and gossip, they leave their children to be watched over by the helpers and when they have had enough, they collect up their children and are off. Messy cups and untidy room left in their wake! The assumption is that others exist to serve them! Few ever want to help with the mundane and humble task of clearing up. Yet this is where Christ is found!

It is interesting how different the Gospel of St John, written about 95AD, is from the other three. He seems to assume that his readers already have a knowledge of at least one of the other Gospels. John, for example, presents a unique and theological approach to the divine origin of the Christ, at the beginning of his account of the Good News. His Last Supper account, in contrast, contains no reference to the Eucharist, but has in its place a memorable and powerful example of humble service.

The evening meal, John tells us (chapter 13:2), was being served. Judas had already planned his betrayal. Jesus was aware of his divine destiny, knowing 'that he had come from God and was returning to God' yet he still got up from the table, took off his outer clothing and tied an apron or towel around his waist. After he had poured water into a basin he began to wash his disciples' feet. He washed the feet of them all – Judas, who was just about to walk out and betray him, and Simon Peter, who later that evening would deny even knowing him! In fact every pair of feet that he washed was going to run away and leave him, in the darkness of the garden, in the hands of his enemies. And still they received a humble service from him!

When Jesus had put the bowl and towel away in the kitchen, he sat down again at the table and said 'Do you understand what I have done for you? You call me "teacher" and "Lord" and rightly so, for that is what I am. Now that I, your Lord and teacher, have washed your feet, you also should wash one another's feet. I have set you an example that you should do what I have done for you.' There it is, humble service; Christ our model.

It costs to be a disciple. In the courageous Dietrich Bonhoeffer's famous book, *The Cost of Discipleship*, he makes a distinction between *cheap grace* and *costly grace*. In other words, he distinguishes between those who call themselves 'Christians' and turn up at church to reap the benefits, but make no further effort to live by Christ's standards; and those who realise that effort, perseverance and dedication are necessary to live by the high standards and values of Jesus, over and above any church attendance. Parishes were full of such people in the late 1930s, when Dietrich Bonhoeffer wrote, against the background of persecution from the Nazis. Many in those days attended weekly service out of a sense of propriety and social expectation. Now considerably fewer attend and more from a sense of personal commitment than seventy years ago; but there are still some churchgoers who want to have their Christianity on the cheap; entirely on their own terms. They worship with others but do not want get involved with them.

The long list of famous Christian heroes since Bonhoeffer, including Maximillian Kolbe (who actually died three years before Bonhoeffer), Martin

Luther King, Chico Mendes, Oscar Romero, Mother Teresa, and others, knew that following Christ and living by his values was costly and could cost not less than everything.

In the first century of Christianity, when Christ's followers were still called 'the People of the Way', the Roman instrument of capital punishment and vicious torture, the cross, was a symbol of terror. Just too many members of the community had known people who had died naked and twisted in agony upon it, or, at the very least, had seen victims crucified by the road side. The cross or the crucifix, which we now recognise as the sign and symbol of Christianity, was not accepted as such until well into the fifth century. It was not until the Second Council of Nicaea, in 787, that the Christian Church officially discussed its important symbolism.

While the public sign of Christianity today may indeed be the cross, the badge of the individual Christian must surely be the apron. Perhaps they are one and the same. To stop behind to clear up after people, at whatever function, week after week, and humbly put on an apron, wash up, sweep the floor and put away the crockery, is to make a sacrifice. To put the service of others, as Christ our Lord did, before our own comfort and convenience, is to make a sacrifice. The cross is supremely the symbol of a loving sacrifice. Christ's humble service at the Last Supper and his torturous death the next day were the same in kind – a sacrifice; but very different in degree. If only all those who wore the cross lived by the cross.

An old headmaster of mine used repeatedly to say, 'those who are faithful in that which is least will be faithful in that which is greater'. I discovered much later that he was quoting from St Luke's Gospel (16:10). 'Boys', he would say, 'be faithful in little things.' Good advice founded on the very example of Jesus himself. If we would be like Christ then the apron is our badge.

**READING:**

Take a few moments, today, to consider all the good things you do for others. This might strike you as inappropriate, because it could seem like an invitation to boast. But it is God who enables you to do what is good, and how can you thank him if you fail to consider the good he has empowered you to do?

In the midst of a world sometimes touched by sin, there are still many people who respond to God's word with a generous heart. They are the ones who make a serious effort to be faithful to their commitments. When they discover people in need, they help them, often at some cost to themselves. They appreciate the joys of life, but they also know how to ask for the strength to bring good out of suffering. Wouldn't observations such as these often describe you? God's grace is powerfully at work in your life too.

Kenneth E. Grabner CSC, *Living Faith*

**PRAYER:**

> Sitting quietly and meditatively, Lord,
> I've been thinking of all the things
> you have given me,
> and all that you do for me.
> I am overcome with the need to say,
> 'thank you, thank you, thank you'.
> The gift of life and health itself,
> the gift of family and friends.
> The gift of faith and a knowledge
> of your wonderful love,
> which knows no bounds.

The good that you do, through me;
and the prayers you answer, for others.
May whatever good I do, with your help,
give you glory and praise.
And may I always be as full of
gratitude, as I feel at this moment.

· 17 ·

## Meeting Christ on the Internet

As travellers cross the English channel, heading for the port of Dover, they see first the famous white cliffs and then, to their right, Dover castle crowning those cliffs. The castle dominates the town in the valley below and for most of my childhood I saw it every day. Born in the town, I grew up with tales about the castle, its secret passageways and the World War II hospital in the cliffs beneath it. I revelled in stories that linked my family to the castle. In my early teens I became an unofficial guide for any family member, friend, acquaintance or visitor to Dover who was interested in visiting it.

It was the Roman *pharos* (lighthouse), next to the church of St Mary-in-the-Castle, which predates the Norman castle by hundreds of years, that particularly fascinated me. Originally there had been a pair of Roman lighthouses, one on each side of the valley port, but the one on the Western Heights (the hills opposite the castle) had been demolished many hundreds of years ago. Standing seventy feet tall, but originally higher, the *pharos* is nothing more than a huge masonry hollow tower in which a vast fire would be lit and kept burning brightly. The two protected fires would act as navigational direction-finders for Roman shipping in the dark or bad weather. Ships leaving France, twenty-one miles away, would aim between the distant lights and find the port: communication by bonfire, simple but very effective. What a long way we have come since those days! At a touch of my finger I can send a message up to a satellite circling the earth and then, in seconds, on to Australia or any part of the world I choose.

According to established practice I am not supposed to tell you this, but part of my Internet password is *'pharos'*! It is easy to link the concept of the *pharos*, the fiery lighthouse guiding ships in the dark or a storm, to Christ, the light of the world.

The following appeared in a popular tabloid daily newspaper as a prediction for the new millennium:

> *The Internet has given power to the individual. That power is based on knowledge. In the twenty-first century, those who know will do. Those who do, will succeed.* (lst January 2000)

How does a Christian, a friend and follower of Christ, view such a prediction? Whatever our initial thoughts about such a secular prophecy, there is no doubt that the Internet is here to stay and of the greatest importance for our age. The benefits are many; just recently I heard, for example, how the Othona Christian Community, at Bradwell, Essex, has doubled its support and membership through having their details and programme available on the Internet.

There are some key words used in the newspaper prophecy: *individual, power, knowledge, succeed.* Not all news regarding the Internet is good news. Concern has been expressed by specialists in human development and education about the isolation of young people, who spend many hours a week at their computers, playing individual games and 'chatting' on the Internet. ('Chat' is defined in Internet parlance as 'a live conversation with any number of other people anywhere in the world'.) There is more to effective and creative communication than typing words to appear on someone's screen, wherever in the world that person may be. We are created by God to be present to one another, to be social beings, living out our lives in communities, with opportunities to love and respect one another. Love will not grow and mature if an Internet 'relationship' which is not totally to one's liking, can be terminated by the touch of a key on a keyboard.

Is any genuine Christian seeking *power*? The words we associate with Christ are *love, service, humility, sacrifice*. None of these associate easily with the word *power*, which infers domination, control and superiority. Jesus was not a powerful man in any of these senses. His power came from his revealing message, direct from his Father: the love he inspired, the example of humble service which he gave. It is true that God worked miracles through Jesus to illustrate and confirm the message of love and show that the Messiah was 'Lord of Creation' (the calming of the storm and the other nature miracles), but these were never exhibitions of domination and superiority.

The sheer volume of facts available on and through the Internet is mind-blowing. At the time of Jesus there was a vast library at Alexandria, in Egypt, with a collection of over 100,000 books. It survived until the end of the third century, so it is not just our age that considers it important to store knowledge and information. It was at Alexandria, in the mid-second century (so about one hundred years after Christ) that the first Christian institute of higher learning was established, led by the famous Christian writers, Clement and Origen. Of course, one of the big differences between the library at Alexandria and the Internet is the accessibility to the general public of information from around the world in one's own home, school or office. (In passing, the *pharos* at Alexandria was one of the seven wonders of the world.)

Did Jesus know about the Alexandrian library? Yes, almost certainly; because Greek traders passing through Galilee, on the great road from Egypt to the north, would probably have boasted of it. As a Jew it would have been of little interest to him, simply because it was Greek and every good Jew believed that all necessary knowledge and wisdom was to be found in the Scriptures and the rabbinical writings.

In proclaiming the Gospel of Christ, St Paul debated with a group of Epicurean and Stoic philosophers (Acts 17:18) in Athens. Luke, the writer of Acts, makes an aside (verse 21): 'all the Athenians and the foreigners who lived there spent their time doing nothing but talking about and listening to the latest ideas.' Nothing changes, does it! The Internet is used for this very purpose by many people. Young people, especially, spend an inordinate amount of time 'chatting' on-line about the latest ideas, fashions etc.

Does having an almost limitless volume of information and knowledge, available to us at our finger tips, make us better persons? To know is not necessarily to do. For example, there are many drivers who know that it is dangerous to exceed the speed limit, in a built-up area, but they still drive too fast and put people's lives at risk. Young people are constantly warned about the dangers of smoking and drug taking, but they do it in ever increasing numbers. To know is not to do, because we are flawed human beings. If we are wise we do not damage our bodies with an excess of anything.

There is a difference between 'knowledge' and 'wisdom'. The Internet will give us knowledge, but not wisdom. That is a gift of God.

In the composite canticle which includes the prayer of Solomon, found in the Book of Wisdom we read:

> 'Give me the wisdom that sits by your throne,
> and do not reject me from among your servants…
> …for even if one is perfect among the sons
>     of men,
> yet without the wisdom that comes from you
> he will be regarded as nothing' (Wis 9:4-6).

Even if one were able to carry in one's head all the knowledge that is to be found on the Internet, yet, without the wisdom that comes from God, it would be worthless. God knows everything and is wisdom itself;

> 'she is a breath of the power of God,
> pure emanation of the glory of the Almighty;
> so nothing impure can find its way into her.
> For she is a reflection of the eternal light,
> untarnished mirror of God's active power,
> and image of his goodness' (Wis 7:24-25).

Is not Christ the 'image of God's goodness'? Those words remind us of the opening of the Gospel according to John;

> 'In the beginning was the Word, the Word was with God and the Word was God' (Jn 1:1).

It is almost as though (and human words can only approximate to divine truth) God spoke all his knowledge – that is, all there is to know – in one single word. Since God is Truth, all his knowledge would be a mirror image of himself. The Word would be himself. It would be Wisdom, who was with God in the beginning (Wis 9:9). John the Evangelist continues his prologue:

> 'He was with God in the beginning.
> Through him all things came into being,
> not one thing came into being except through him' (1:3).

And a little later (verse 14):

> 'The Word became flesh,
> he lived among us,
> and we saw his glory,
> the glory that he has from the Father
> as only Son of the Father,
> full of grace and truth.'

Christ is the Knowledge and the Wisdom of God. The Internet provides us with knowledge but we are required to use that knowledge with wisdom.

Not long ago, I was present in a small group that was meeting with our local bishop when he made a comment that has remained with me. 'Remember,' he said, 'we are not called to be successful; we are called to be faithful.' Our world rates people according to their success in life; God rates us according to our faithfulness. If the Internet helps us to be more faithful as Christians, as employers and employees, as partners and parents, as teachers and students, as children and young people, then we and the Internet will be successful.

**READING:**

The human spirit hungers for knowledge – for entire, integral knowledge. Nothing can destroy our longing to know, and naturally our ultimate craving is for knowledge of Primordial Being, of Whom or What actually exists. All down the ages man has paid instinctive homage to this First Principle. Our fathers and forefathers reverenced Him in different ways because they did not know him 'as he is' (1 Jn 3:2). Some (surely they were among the wisest) set up an altar with this inscription, 'To the unknown god' (Acts 17:23) Even in our day we are continually made aware that reason *per se* cannot advance us over the threshold to the 'Unknown'. God is our only means of access to this higher knowledge if he will reveal himself.

Archimandrite Sophrony, *His Life is Mine*

**PRAYER:**

As I key in my password,
which momentarily reminds me of you,
Light of the World,
I'm still so new at all this, that I'm amazed.
To be connected, through lots of networks,
with so much potential knowledge and information!
It's awesome, and such a tribute to human
    inventiveness.
But do I really need it? How am I going to use it?
Will I be a better, holier person, for being computer
    literate?
Since you are the Truth, Lord,
will I know you better, through using the Internet?
Surely I need to pray for the gift of wisdom,
that I may use well this incredible work of human
    ingenuity.
May my work for others benefit;
may I not waste time and money,
idly 'chatting' and gossiping to no purpose.
May I appreciate the skills of those
who make the Internet work, and continually develop it.
May mankind's inventiveness bring glory
to you, the Light of the World.

## · 18 ·

## MEETING CHRIST IN CHILDREN'S BOOKS

Saying night prayers and reading to your young children at bedtime is one of the most satisfying of parental duties. It is well-known that young children like to hear the same story over and over again. It is not so well-known (because parents do the recounting) that tired-out parents quite often fall asleep on the job! At least I did!

My eldest daughter, to whom I spent many happy hours reading, is now a primary school teacher. She tells me that the famous Ladybird books that she enjoyed at night-time are no longer used in the classroom. In our home we still have shelves full of them; some so well-worn that their covers are missing. *The Princess and the Frog, The Golden Goose* and *The Enormous Turnip* were firm favourites. Children have no problems with talking frogs, or wizen old men like Rumplestiltskin. Such stories have been around for thousands of years, as witness the Bible with its talking snake, in Genesis, chapter 3, and Balaam's talking donkey, in Numbers, chapter 22.

Long before writing was invented stories were in circulation, used to convey moral teaching and pass on to the next generation the beliefs and values of the tribe or people. In a story like *The Princess and the Frog* a very spiritual message can be found. The frog is really a handsome prince, who is under an evil spell. He can only be saved by the kiss of a beautiful princess. The wicked witch has assumed that no woman in her right mind, let alone a royal princess, is going to kiss an ugly, repulsive frog. The princess is so good, however, that she puts aside her own feelings and kisses the frog. She does not know, it should be noted, what the outcome will be, namely, a handsome prince is going to be released, to love and marry. It is by unselfishly embracing the ugly and repulsive that salvation is found. Christ touched hideously deformed lepers and spent time in the company of the marginalised of his society. He embraced the horrors of rejection, scourging, crowning with thorns and crucifixion to win our salvation. Mother Teresa picking up the ugly, deformed lepers, dying on the streets of Calcutta, comes to mind. As does the work of the Simon Community and others, who give up a night's sleep to take hot soup and bread to the homeless, sleeping in the doorways of our big cities.

There is a simpler spiritual message in *The Golden Goose*. The strong and intelligent sons of a woodcutter, each in turn, refuse to help an old man who is hungry and thirsty: they all have accidents. The youngest son, who is a simpleton, is sent out to complete their work. He generously shares his food and drink with the old man and is rewarded with the golden goose. He uses the goose, not to enrich himself, but to put people who need help in touch with one another. As a result he ends up winning the hand of the princess.

*The Enormous Turnip* has another Christian message. An old farmer goes out to pull up the turnips in his field. One is enormous. He pulls and pulls and cannot raise it. He gets his wife to help, but together they cannot move the turnip. They enlist their son and then their daughter, but to no avail. The dog joins the line that is pulling at the turnip and still it does not budge. The cat helps but still they are unsuccessful. Finally, a tiny mouse is invited to help and, this time, up comes the turnip. They all carry it into the kitchen and share a turnip dinner. Here is the wonderful teaching of Christ that the smallest person matters. The most insignificant can transform life; and so can working together as a team, in community.

Another series of books that the children loved was the 'Mr Men' stories by Roger Hargreaves. There is a long list of characters, including Mr Silly who lives in Nonsense Land, Mr Happy who is fat and round and happy, Mr Fussy who spends all day and every day re-arranging his furniture, and many others. Mr Topsy-Turvy was my special favourite; he wore his hat upside down and everything in his house worked back-to-front.

Mr Topsy-Turvy reminds me of Jesus and his message. In a sense, Jesus is Mr Topsy-Turvy and his friends and followers are called to assume a topsy-turvy way of life. The widely accepted values of the world are not the values of Christ and his disciples.

I recently read a short article by a friend of mine in *The Tablet*. Fr John Glynn, composer of many well-known hymns, like 'I watch the sunrise', wrote of the wonderful and inspiring experience of his trek through the Sinai desert, sleeping out under the stars, the climb up Mount Sinai and the visit to St Catherine's Orthodox monastery at the foot of the mountain. When he described how he felt on his return to 'civilisation' and 'normality', I immediately empathised; I knew exactly what he was talking about. Only months before I'd had a similar experience.

My adventure was simpler and less exciting – on

the coast-to-coast walk. My daughter, Angela, and I walked, scrambled and climbed 120 miles in seven days: from one side of the Lake District to the other and over the Pennines to Richmond in North Yorkshire. We met and talked to only a handful of people, rarely saw a car and the other trappings of modern life. We travelled through mile after mile of beautiful and unspoilt countryside and struggled with the elements. Returning on the train, I felt remote and withdrawn from the other passengers. Standing outside Southend Victoria station, waiting for my wife to come and collect us in the car, I could hardly believe the violent rush and noise of the traffic haring round the roundabout outside. Swirling round my feet was an eddy of litter and wastepaper. I felt disorientated, and thought 'is this civilisation?'

    I wandered back into the station to the shop, to catch a glimpse of the world news from the headlines of the racked newspapers. What event of national or international importance had we missed while away? I stared with disbelief at the headline on virtually every newspaper. Most expressed the vital news with a question: *Will Ginger Spice leave the Spice Girls?* So this is what concerns the people of our society! This is civilisation! Welcome back, I thought, to the topsy-turvy world of normality and what passes for culture and human values. (I later learnt that the day before my experience at the news stand in the station forecourt, the most violent war since the Second World War had begun in Ethiopia, killing tens of thousands of people. But that did not merit even a mention in our popular press.)

We read, at the beginning of the Gospels, that Jesus left society and normal life behind and went out into the desert. He slept under the stars and experienced the starkness of the barren, stony landscape. He was away, by himself, for a long period of time. When he returned he began his teaching; and he taught that the values of Jewish society, at that time, were topsy-turvy.

What were those values? Jewish society viewed religion as at the very centre of life; it informed and shaped everything that the Jews did and how they did it. (How different from today's secular society where religion is treated as a pastime banished to the fringes of modern life.) Everything that happened to you had a religious significance and interpretation. If you became ill or caught a disease, you became a leper or were born blind, that was a punishment from God for wrong doing. You, or your parents, must have sinned (see Jn 9:2). If you were rich, that was a blessing from God and you were therefore one of God's special favourites; however, if you were poor the opposite applied, you were of no interest to God. Jewish males, since they were specially dedicated to God at birth and, through circumcision, bore the sign of the Covenant on their bodies, were far superior to women. So life was fine if you were male, fit and well, and wealthy. The marginalised of society were the women, the poor and the sick. It was to these that Christ directed his special love and attention.

Humanly speaking, it was probably his time in the desert that gave Jesus the insight to see how topsy-turvy society was. This revelation directed the whole of his teaching and brought down upon him the hatred of the privileged classes. It was the fit, wealthy males of the religious establishment that plotted his downfall.

A collected summary of Jesus' teaching is found in chapters 5-7 of Matthew's Gospel. It opens with the Beatitudes and the words *Blessed are the poor in spirit.*

Luke (6:20) has a more stark version, *Blessed are you who are poor.* It is balanced by the contrasting words: *Woe to you who are rich* (verse 24). It continues with Christ's words *Blessed are you who hunger now* which are contrasted with *Woe to you who are well-fed now.* The words are crystal clear; there can be no doubt whose side Christ is on.

Little has changed. Our world still says, *Blessed are those who become rich and acquire all the latest products and wear the latest fashions.*

It says, *Blessed are those who are assertive and push themselves forward and get noticed.* Jesus, our Mr Topsy-Turvy, says *Blessed are the meek.* And so it continues. The values of Jesus are not the values of the world.

St John's Gospel is full of warnings about the topsy-turvy values of 'the world' from the opening, 'the light [of Christ] shines in the darkness, but the darkness has never understood it'; to the words of Jesus in chapter 17: 'I have given them [his followers] your word and the world has hated them, for they are not of the world any more than I am of the world. My prayer is not that you take them out of the world, but that you protect them from the evil one. They are not of the world, even as I am not of it. Sanctify them by the truth' (verse 16).

**READING:**
In order to listen well, silence is needful; it is needful that we should often, like Jesus at the Transfiguration, go apart into a solitary place. Certainly Jesus is to be found elsewhere, even in the turmoil of great cities but he is only heard well in a peaceful soul surrounded by an atmosphere of silence. He is only understood in a soul that prays.

It is then above all that he reveals himself to the soul, drawing her to him and transfiguring her in him.

Columba Marmion, *'Christ in His Mysteries'*

**PRAYER:**

I miss reading at bedtime,
to one or other of my children.
Face glowing after a bath and all expectant,
while we both got comfortable
and found the right page.
Lord, childhood passes so quickly.
But you would have us all remain childlike –
not childish, of course; childlike
in our trust and confidence in you.
Not necessarily successful, but faithful.
Your values, not highly regarded by this world;
but necessary for the next.
We find them difficult to hang on to,
in our brash and materialistic society.
In fact we can't, without your help, Lord.
So in your love, please give us a helping hand.

# · 19 ·

# MEETING CHRIST AT SUNDAY FOOTBALL

Last season I very nearly got a red card! I didn't think it possible, until the trouble occurred, now I know differently. I have been much better behaved this season! It happened like this. My son's team, Shoebury Boys Under-15s, was playing away. The match was arranged for 11 a.m., but through a communications error the team had been told that the kick-off time was 10 a.m. We arrived at 9.30 a.m., discovered our mistake and then hung around on an exposed and windy February field. At last the home side, Rayleigh Rovers, arrived; but then there was no referee. We were assured that he was on his way and told to wait. At 11.15 a.m. a group of our parents, rather irately suggested that we proceed with one of our number refereeing. This had just been agreed when the referee arrived. The match got underway twenty minutes late.

Almost unbelievably, after half an hour of play, the referee was struck forcibly, but accidentally, by the ball. He limped off in pain, declaring that he could not continue! (Now you have to understand that there is a degree of ritual involved at weekend football; the customary practice is for the parents of one team to stand on the opposite side of the field, the opposite line, to the other. There are good personal safety reasons for this!) Without consultation with the Shoebury Boys' parents, the manager of the other side took over the role of referee. There was muttering from our side about this; and I was not silent!

In the second half, when we were one goal down, a pass from a Rayleigh Rovers defender to one of their forwards was deflected off the referee, who did not get out of the way in time. Instead he stepped into the path of our defender; the outcome was that their forward raced through to an undefended goal and scored. I saw red. I am sorry to report that I shouted something rather abusive and not for repetition here! I repeated the accusation that the referee was unfairly helping his team and we stood no chance of a fair match while he was refereeing.

The match was stopped. The referee strode towards our side of the field, straight towards where I, and five other parents were standing. He demanded to know who had shouted out the rude remark… there was a moment of silence; and I looked at my boots! Then there came, from the other parents, a chorus of 'No, Ref. Not us, Ref. You've got it wrong. Sorry, Ref, you couldn't have heard right.' He glowered at us all and said, 'if that happens again, I will clear this line. You will all have to go.' If he had had a red card he would have waved it at this point! He turned, and the match was resumed. When he was well away, the other parents looked at me and, laughing at my embarrassment, said 'You nearly got a red card there.' For the first time I learnt that a referee has authority even over the spectators! Later in the day, when I was warm again and in a better frame of mind, I had to acknowledge, at least to myself, that, whatever the circumstances and provocation, I had no right to pass judgement on the man who had volunteered to take over the job of referee at short notice.

The role of referee, certainly at weekend football, is not an enviable position. I, for one, would not cope well with the aggression and language from some of the players, and their parents! Over the last few years, on most winter and spring Sundays, events on 'the line' have been an eye-opener for me. That hour and a half has been one of the most emotionally highly charged experiences of my week. One minute you are elated at an unexpected goal scored by your side; then you are irritated by what appears to be a bad judgement by the referee or the linesman. Next your defenders do something idiotic and the other side scores! Excitement mounts as your son takes the ball past two or three defenders and looks like scoring; then disappointment for him, when he shoots the ball wide of the goal. Hope as your team is winning, by a small margin, in a cup match, then tension as the other side equals. Pride as your boy heads in a brilliant goal from a corner; anger as a big lad kicks him to the ground and the referee takes no notice.

Until my son, at the age of eight, wanted to join a local club, I had no experience of Sunday football. Once you get involved it dictates the shape of your weekends and, as a family, we have to go to church on Saturday evening. I was amazed at the huge number of boys and young men, plus parents and supporters, who are involved each Sunday. It's not all cheering from the sidelines; when we are playing at home, a small group of us have to put up the goal posts at 8.30 a.m.; which is not much fun on a very frosty or very wet Sunday morning.

The referee has to make instant judgements, and sometimes he or she (some of the best referees are women) gets it wrong. Rather like ourselves in the course of our daily lives. Each day, and repeatedly during the day, we are making judgements. It may be part of our work or it may be in our private or social life. We pass judgement on colleagues' attitudes, their dress sense, the company they keep. We gossip and pass judgement on what others have done, should have done or might do. We may simply just catch sight of someone in the street and before we know it, we are categorising that person: she's a snob or he's a scrounger and a low type.

If we are aiming to be serious disciples of Christ we should have his words ringing in our ears, 'do not judge, or you too will be judged' (Mt 7:1). And in another place Jesus says, 'stop judging by mere appearances and make a right judgement' (Jn 7:24). Human beings do not change; those words would suggest that the problem at the time of Jesus was as real as it is today. Jesus continues in his warning, 'For in the same way as you judge others, you will be judged, and with the measure you use, it will be measured to you.'

The People of the Way, as the first Christians were called, were awaiting the Final Coming of Christ. (They were first called 'Christians', that is 'belonging to Christ' at Antioch some twenty-five years after the first Pentecost Day [see Acts 11:26].) This would involve a final reckoning as well. The Last Judgement was very much more a part of their thinking and prayer life than it is ours. Of course, the expected End of the World did not come for the human race, but it did come for each individual follower of Christ. The End of the World is unlikely to come in my life time, but the end of my world will surely and certainly come. The final Judgement Day may be a long way off, but the end of my life and my own personal meeting with Christ the Judge, will most definitely take place. What will he be seeking? What do judges, and for that matter, referees, seek? Surely it is the truth.

The Jewish rabbi is not, in spite of what most people think, the equivalent of a Christian priest or minister.

The rabbi (from the Hebrew word for 'my teacher') is primarily a teacher and a judge; it is the cantor, who leads the worship on the Sabbath or at the festivals. The rabbi, as a teacher, preaches. He is also an expert in the Law and thereby the local community's judge.

Twice Jesus is addressed as 'Rabbi', on both occasions in St John's Gospel. Everyone knows that Jesus taught, but did he, as a rabbi, pass judgement?

On one occasion ' someone in the crowd said to him, 'Rabbi, tell my brother to divide the inheritance with me.' Jesus replied, 'Man, who appointed me a judge or arbiter between you?' (Lk 12:14). As the Son of Man he has received authority from his Father to judge, 'For as the Father has life in himself, so he has granted the Son to have life in himself. And he has given him authority to judge because he is the Son of Man' (Jn 5:27).

What a referee is trying to see all the time, during the match, is what is actually happening and are the rules being applied and kept. In other words, like a judge in a court of law, he is seeking the truth. On that particular Sunday morning I was not prepared to accept the truth; nor did I have the humility to acknowledge that. At my Final Judgement Christ, the judge, will want to know the truth about me; have I lived by his law of love?

Once a year, I take the Religious Studies A-level group from my school to visit an inspiring Orthodox monastery, tucked away down a narrow Essex lane, not far from Maldon. It is a day out that, over the years, has never failed to lift and inspire me. Sr Magdalene, the nun who always shows us round, has become a good friend. A few years ago we arrived on a June morning, and, as in previous years, Sister was waiting for us. She appeared very subdued. A little later she told us that their founder, Fr Sophrony, who was well into his nineties and resident at the monastery, had died just two weeks before. She told us how the Father Abbot, knowing from the doctors that Fr Sophrony's death was close, went into his room to tell him. The founder listened to the abbot and then said, 'I am sorry but you are wrong, Father, I am not humble enough yet to die!'

What is humility? I like the definition of Fr Carey-Elwes: 'Humility is the truth about ourselves loved.' Also that of St Vincent de Paul: 'The reason why God is so great a lover of humility is because he is the great lover of truth. Now humility is nothing but truth, while pride is nothing but lying.'

Humility then is more about acknowledging the truth about ourselves, rather than putting ourselves down. It is to do with seeing ourselves, as far as possible, from God's eyes. In the Orthodox Church Fr Sophrony was, and still is, highly respected as a great spiritual guide and director of souls. If he saw a link between dying and meeting Christ the judge and the need for great humility, then that merits much thought.

On her deathbed, St Thérèse of Lisieux, in dreadful pain, asked her Superior to help her prepare for death. 'You are prepared', she was told. She answered, 'Yes, it seems that I have ever only sought the truth. Yes, I have understood humility of heart. It seems to me I am humble' (*Spirituality* p.34 no.28).

**READING:**

My mind is made to see God, and I am always looking at myself. Humility comes to correct my vision. And the first thing that humility tells me is that I have nothing of myself. It does not say that I have nothing at all, but that I have nothing through myself. I do not exist of myself, and nothing that I have comes of myself. Neither my existence, nor any of the gifts of existence in me, is through myself. What I have of myself is nothing.

Humility, which is truth, makes me see and recognise the nothingness which I am of myself. It does not frown at the lessons of its own nothingness, which are given to man in so many of his experiences and in so many shapes. To acknowledge one's sins and mistakes, not to persist in one's own views, to admit one's imperfections and shortcomings, to accept inward and outward humiliations, to draw conclusions preferably against oneself and in favour of others, etc, this is what is suggested by humility. True humility neither misjudges, nor denies, nor lessens any of God's gifts. It too well understands the responsibility for talents received. It recognises natural gifts and supernatural gifts, and knows whence they come. And when these gifts, which are recognised by it and used owing to it, yield their fruits, it knows that these fruits are to be attributed to the Giver of the gifts that yield them. It sees so clearly that it has nothing which it has not received, and it takes good care not to glory in them as if it had not received them (1 Cor 4:7).

Joseph Tissot, *'The Interior Life'*

**PRAYER:**
>Why, Lord, do we humans
>find it so hard to say, genuinely, 'I'm sorry'?
>That first sin of Adam and Eve is to blame –
>a sin of pride.
>Now pride comes so easily and naturally to us;
>but humility is a grace and a gift of God.
>You, Lord, were the second Adam,
>humble where he was proud,
>obedient where he was disobedient.
>Thank you for your inspiring example of humility.
>Thank you for your obedience;
>which took you to death on a cross.
>May I receive your grace to be humble.
>May I seek your will in my life.

## · 20 ·

## Meeting Christ Under the Stars

A recent advertisement in my daily newspaper read: *Name A Star: millions of stars remain unnamed. Now, as a gift, you can name a star from only £49.* The advertisement continued with the words, *Have your star name in the constellation of your choice. Your star name will be permanently recorded on our register.* The eye-catching advertisement concluded, significantly, with these words: *naming a star is symbolic rather than scientific.*

It seemed to me, a casual reader of the newspaper, that for your money all that you would get would be the star name of your choice, along with your own name, added to a list placed in the company's filing cabinet, or rather, computer memory bank. A totally worthless activity, for by what authority did this commercial enterprise parcel out the universe and, if the astronomers of the world were not to be informed of my selection and naming, what actually would be the point?

One problem teases me a little. What if there is intelligent life somewhere out there on a planet going round a star (sun) in a far-away galaxy? Youngsters, I find, are fond of the thought of 'aliens', an idea constantly fed by weird and wonderful films and TV programmes. On this subject they are reluctant to accept the current findings of science. At the present time there is not one scrap of scientific evidence to show that there is intelligent life anywhere else in the whole universe. As far as we know, we are alone in the vastness of the universe. But just suppose the opposite is shown to be true and we find other intelligent life forms. The question that teases me is, has Christ been to them?

According to traditional beliefs the human race fell into sin and Christ came to redeem us. Now if there are other intelligent beings, are they sinless or have they sinned? If they are sinless does that mean that they do not know Christ, and would we sinners be allowed to mix with them? If they have sinned, like us, has Christ been to them too? And how was that managed? Is there a real issue here, or not?

One thing is for certain: there is no comparable experience to standing, on a clear night, out in a wide open space, away from city lights, and gazing at the stars. Such an awesome experience has been soul-searching and humbling for humans since the first human eye opened and looked at the world. Perhaps it is even more mind-boggling for modern humans since, as we gaze, we are aware of the utter immeasurable vastness that we are looking up and into. Science tells us that our solar system – a star (the sun) with nine planets – is tucked away in a corner of the Milky Way galaxy. Our galaxy has between 100 and 200 billion stars, many with their own planetary systems! The wonder of it all does not stop there. The astronomers inform us that there are a similar number of stars in each of the other trillion galaxies! Who can even begin to imagine that! The numbers involved, once you start talking and thinking about the universe, are so mind-blowingly vast. The experts point out that so huge a number of galaxies means that there are 20 galaxies (each with about 100 billion stars) for each human person on earth!

It all seems just too much... too hard to imagine; and too remote and impersonal. The Bible puts a more personal slant on it, telling us that it is God who determines all this and knows each planet, star and galaxy by name.

> 'God determines the number of the stars and calls each by name' (Ps 147:4).

Although the Psalms were written hundreds of years before Jesus used them, they reflect the cosmology and the simple beliefs that were current in his time.

> 'By his word the heavens were made,
> by the breath of his mouth all the stars' (Ps 32:4).

These words call to mind the text of the First Creation story in Genesis, chapter one.

Just as they believed that God was responsible for people being rich or poor, well or sick, so the contemporaries of Jesus believed that God was responsible for the thunder and the lightning:

> 'The voice of the Lord strikes with flashes of lightning.
> The voice of the Lord shakes the desert....
> The voice of the Lord twists the oaks
> And strips the forest bare' (Ps 28[29]:7-9).

We scientifically educated people of the twenty-first century forget that most of the people who have lived upon planet earth believed that it was flat! Jesus too, being a man of his time, would have believed the world was flat. His divinity did not take away his naturally acquired human knowledge.

One of the traditional images of the Resurrection is the butterfly. Early in Christian thought the parallel between the caterpillar entering the 'tomb' of the chrysalis, then appearing transformed as the beautiful butterfly and the wonder of the Resurrection, was evident to all. The torn and tortured body of the man, Jesus, was laid in the darkness of the tomb and on the third day the glorified Christ appeared among his friends. In the very first Christian sermon (Acts 2:14-40) Peter tells the crowd, 'God has made this Jesus, whom you crucified, both Lord and Christ' (Acts 2:36).

In the following months and years the community of believers thought and prayed about the Resurrection, and the Pentecost event. Their understanding and beliefs grew. It was the Apostle Paul who recognised and expressed, for the first time, the sublimity of Christ's position and role.

> 'He is the image of the invisible God, the firstborn over all creation. For by him all things were created: things in heaven and on earth, visible and invisible, whether thrones or powers or rulers or authorities; all things were created by him and for him. He is before all things, and in him all things hold together' (Col 1:15-17).

Christ, Paul says, is the head of all creation. All those planets, stars and galaxies were 'created by him and for him'. When we look up, at night-time, and behold the wonder of the heavens, it is Christ's glory that we behold. Of all the epiphanies (manifestations) of God, the wonders of the universe are the first and most magnificent. From the 'big bang', some twenty billion years ago and the vibrant activity of the two elements, hydrogen and helium, from which all has evolved, to the 'twenty-first-century's scientific discovery of the human genome, God is revealed. The primary revelation, long before biblical times, is up there in the night sky; and Christ is Lord of it all!

**READING:**

I do not know when I have had happier times in my soul, than when I have been sitting at work, with nothing before me but a candle and a white cloth, and hearing no sound but that of my own breath, with God in my soul and heaven in my eye... I rejoice in being exactly what I am – a creature capable of loving God, and who, as long as God lives must be happy. I get up and look for a while out of the window, and gaze at the moon and stars, the work of an Almighty hand. I think of the grandeur of the universe, and then sit down, and think myself one of the happiest beings in it.

A Poor Methodist Woman, quoted in<br>*The Perfection of Love*

**PRAYER:**

> When I think, Almighty God,
> – and it's hard to think –
> of the utter vastness of your creation,
> I am filled with awe and amazement.
> That the universe is from you,
> and held in being by you,
> I do not doubt; but it's size!
> If this is what you can make,
> how awesome must you be!
> I, a tiny creature from your hand,
> worship and adore you.
> Wonder is heaped upon wonder.
> For Christ, who dwells within me,
> and knows me and loves me,
> is the head of all you have created.
> So, with a little more confidence,
> I adore you, with him, and through him.
> From within me, may he offer you,
> unending glory, honour and praise.

# Afterword

On the road to Emmaus the two disciples failed, at first, to recognise Christ, their friend (Lk 24:13ff). Yet he was really with them. Most of the time, we, Christ's friends of the twenty-first century, suffer from the same blindness. It isn't that Christ is not present to us; we are just too preoccupied coping with the cares and pressures of life. It is not a fault, as such, more a loss of opportunity. It is a simple matter of spiritual blindness. If we could 'see', we would develop a much richer and rewarding relationship with Christ. We all need to say, with blind Bartimaeus, 'Rabbi, I want to see' (Mk 10:51).

Composing this book in my spare time has helped me to see a little more clearly. If it helps other friends of Christ to do the same, it will have achieved its purpose. I've put this book together in the midst of a busy family life; sometimes with young children at my feet or wanting a 'go' on the word processor! Constantly interrupted and called away, on average three or four times every half an hour, it has been difficult to keep the continuity of the text – and, at times, my patience! My own four children are in their teens or twenties, all living at home (not a large place), with their own friends popping in and out. My wife is a child-minder with two or three under-fives at any one time under her wing (and sometimes under my feet!). Mostly it is joyously active and noisy, but not conducive to the writing of meditative material. It must be wonderful to write in a quiet study or in the solitude of a religious house; but those are privileges beyond my reach. Perhaps this family background and setting has been a more 'real' context in which to write for ordinary lay people.

This book is populated by people, for Christ is for, with and within people. He is not primarily to be found in dogmatic statements, spiritual tenets or official documents. Long before any article of doctrine was written down, Christ told us where to look for him, 'where two or three come together in my name, there am I with them' (Mt 18:20).

Stories have been used throughout, because it was the effective method of Jesus himself and, as he knew, everyone enjoys a good story. It has been the 'message' of each story that has mattered; apart from members of my family, the names of people, and some of the settings, have been changed. This book is not intended to be read from cover to cover, but reflectively, over a period of time. For example, the twenty chapters could be spread over Lent, dividing each chapter in half.

It also tries to address, a little, one of the most frequently-heard heresies of modern times; namely that Jesus of Nazareth taught that we should love one another. You hear this constantly, in schools, from staff and pupils, in prayer groups and even in Sunday homilies. That was never the teaching of Jesus. He actually said, in answer to the question 'which is the greatest commandment?': 'Love the Lord your God with all your heart and with all your soul and with all your mind. The second commandment is like it: 'Love your neighbour as yourself' (Mt 22:37, Lk 10:27 etc).

Either commandment, without the other, presents an unbalanced teaching. (And the point of the Good

Samaritan parable, found in Luke's Gospel, is that the two Jews, who passed by, were so wrapped up in their love of God, that they neglected their neighbour.) While it is true that we find God in our neighbour and love him present there, the effort must equally be made to love God directly with all our heart, soul and mind, in all that we do.